BRAIN OF BRITAIN

BRAIN OF BRITAIN

a quiz book from the BBC radio programme

John P Wynn

British Broadcasting Corporation

Published by the British Broadcasting Corporation,
35 Marylebone High Street, London W1M 4AA

ISBN 0 563 12199 8

First published 1972

Printed in England by John Blackburn Ltd
Old Run Road, Leeds LS10 2AA

Contents

Questions

Answers

Introduction

In the simplest terms, a quiz is basically 'Question' and 'Answer'. But the art of a successful quiz show is the format into which question and answer is put. And in *Brain of Britain*, John P. Wynn devised one such format. For there is certainly no doubt that *Brain of Britain* is one of the most popular of radio quiz programmes, with an audience of millions in the United Kingdom and throughout the world.

The programme started life some twenty years ago as 'What Do You Know?'; the title was changed to *Brain of Britain* in 1968. And John P. Wynn has compiled and set the questions for every series; some 20,000 questions would be a fairly conservative estimate!

Joan Clark (later to become Mrs Wynn) produced the first and subsequent series until her retirement from the BBC in 1970. 'Quiz-Queen of Radio' was no misnomer for Joan, whose experience and expertise was unrivalled in this particular genre.

The voice of *Brain of Britain* was Franklin Engelmann; he compèred the programmes from the very beginning until his death in March 1972. He will always be remembered with deep affection for his unique personal and professional qualities—qualities that made him an ideal chairman. His obvious enjoyment of the competition communicated itself to listener and contestant alike.

As in any competition, attention will naturally be focussed on the contestants, and their progress. For instance, from an original entry of 56 contestants from all parts of the United Kingdom, the new 'Brain of Britain' will have won through four rounds of the quiz, and answered correctly some seventy to eighty questions over a wide area of general knowledge.

There is no easy way to the title—and while competition is always friendly, it is also keen. One thing is certain—whoever wins the title 'Brain of Britain' deserves to win it.

John Fawcett Wilson, Producer

Quiz One

General Knowledge

1 If the Romans did not call the potato 'spuddus murphii', what did they call it?

2 Do you know how the potato acquired the slang name of a 'murphy'?

3 Who or what, precisely, was the Khedive?

4 The constellation *Ursa Major* is called the Plough, the Great Bear and Charles's Wain. Who was Charles?

5 What did 'Friendship', 'Aurora', 'Sigma' and 'Faith' have in common?

6 What is, or was, Tulipomania? A serious outbreak actually took place in Europe in 1634.

7 If a shop assistant told you: 'We have a nice length of Kidderminster here, sir', what would he be talking about?

8 What do the letters DPH mean after someone's name?

9 What do we call what the Romans called *Propontis*?

10 The well-known Charterhouse School was founded in 1611 by Thomas Sutton on the site of a Carthusian monastery in Smithfield, London. It removed to the country in 1872. Can you say where?

11 To whom would Lulsgate, Rhoose, Yeadon and Woolsington have a particular significance, and why?

12 What special knowledge would a Hebraist have?

Quiz One

Words

1 Is a hidalgo a Spanish dance, a Moorish dwelling, an official at a bullfight, a Portuguese cloak, or what else is it?

2 Who or what was a virgate?

3 What is photometry?

4 An incubus is now an oppressive influence, a mental burden. What did it mean previously?

5 What is the literal meaning of a hieroglyphic?

6 A regicide is the murderer of a king; a fratricide is the murderer of a brother. What was a barmecide?

7 A shibboleth is now held to mean an old-fashioned and generally abandoned doctrine. What was a shibboleth originally?

8 Today, to say 'the place was a shambles' means it was a bit of a mess or muddle. What was the original meaning of shambles?

9 What is jactitation of marriage?

10 What was the difference between a ferrule and a ferule?

11 What is the connection between a little mouse and your upper arm?

12 Is solipsism a grammatical error, sun-spot activity, an intense desire to be alone, the floral peculiarity of following the sun, as the sunflower, or what else is it?

Quiz One
Geography

1 In which Scottish county is Glencoe?

2 The Rivers Don and Dee both flow through the same county. Can you identify the county?

3 Spalding is famous for its bulb farming. It is situated in the south of Holland. Is there anything wrong with this statement? If so, what?

4 Whereabouts would you expect to see the Merry Men of May performing?

5 Can you name one of the four largest Shetland Islands?

6 The defeat of the Royalists at Naseby in June 1645 was the decisive battle of the Civil War. In which county is Naseby?

7 If you read the following in a local paper, would you consider it accurate? And why, or why not? *Dorchester was formerly the Roman station of Dorocina. It became an important town in Saxon times and before the Norman Conquest was the Cathedral City of the largest diocese in England. It is in Oxfordshire, on the River Thames.*

8 What area of England is known as the Hardy country?

9 How many counties are there in Wales (excluding Monmouthshire)?

10 Which is the most easterly county in the British Isles?

11 Can you name the bridge over the River Thames nearest to its mouth?

12 In which county does the longest river in the United Kingdom rise?

Quiz One

History

1 Chamberlain – Churchill – Attlee – Eden – Macmillan – Wilson – Heath. Who is missing?

2 In which year did the Labour Party first form a Government in this country?

3 Which Ministry did Lord Robens occupy in Mr Attlee's Government from April – October 1951?

4 Who was Germany's Chancellor immediately before Hitler came to power in 1933?

5 Who preceded Herr Willy Brandt as Federal Chancellor of West Germany?

6 Who was the first Prime Minister of India?

7 What was the name of the Czech mining village, completely destroyed by the Nazis in 1942 as a reprisal for the assassination of Reinhard Heydrich?

8 During the Second World War what was 'Operation Dynamo'?

9 Can you remember precisely when V.E. Day was?

10 Can you say, to within a year, when the Parliament, which first met on 26 November 1935 under Stanley Baldwin, was dissolved?

11 Seven of the following eight men were Prime Ministers of Britain: Joseph Chamberlain, A. J. Balfour, Bonar Law, Ramsay MacDonald, Stanley Baldwin, Neveille Chamberlain, Henry Campbell-Bannerman and Sir Alec Douglas-Home. Who is the odd man out?

12 Who was Deputy Supreme Commander of the Allied Expeditionary Force, under General Eisenhower, from 1943–45?

Quiz One

People

1 Edson Arantes do Nascimento is a famous sportsman. As whom is he better known?

2 As whom was Mrs Kennerley Rumford better known?

3 What was the title of the eldest son of King Edward VII?

4 He was a Triple Blue at Oxford (Cricket, Soccer and Athletics); took first-class Honours in Classical Moderations; held the long-jump World Record for eleven years; got a full International cap for England at Soccer; made over 30,000 runs in first-class cricket, during which time he captained England against Australia. Subsequently he commanded a boys' training ship, and is said to have refused the crown of Albania. Who was he?

5 As whom was the Canadian, William Maxwell Aitken, better known after 1917?

6 As whom was Lev D. Bronstein better known?

7 Who married Nadezhda Krupskaya in 1898?

8 What was the name of Mussolini's son-in-law who was the Italian Foreign Minister at the outbreak of the Second World War?

9 For what is Jean Anouilh best known?

10 How did the Piccard twins become famous?

11 Which British missionary, originally a parlour-maid, went to China in 1930, became a naturalised Chinese known as *Ai-weh-deh* (the Virtuous One), spied for China in the Sino-Japanese War, and made her name world-famous by leading a hundred children to safety across the mountains to Thailand?

12 For what is Mrs Mary Baker Eddy remembered?

Quiz One

Literature

1 Of which unpleasant institution was Wackford Squeers in charge?

2 Which famous British actor, playwright (and producer), author of *Night Must Fall* and *The Corn is Green,* published his autobiography in 1961, entitled *George,* his own unused first christian name?

3 How did the 'Ancient Mariner' kill the albatross?

4 Who was responsible for the lines:
Laugh, and the world laughs with you;
Weep, and you weep alone?

5 Who said, according to whom:
Sink me the ship, Master Gunner – sink her, split her in twain!
Fall into the hands of God, not into the hands of Spain!?

6 Can you identify Anne Brontë's *Tenant of Wildfell Hall*?

7 In which country did Gulliver meet the Struldbrugs?

8 What was the name of the itinerant concert party, whose adventures were described by a North-Country author in a best-selling novel published in 1929?

9 Who or what are or were the Older Edda and the Younger Edda?

10 What is the connection between the play *The Chiltern Hundreds* and a former Prime Minister?

11 You know who Sir Christopher Wren was, who lived from 1632–1723. But do you know how Percival Christopher Wren (1885–1941) made his name?

12 For what historical reason did W. C. Sellar and R. J. Yeatman go into partnership?

Quiz One

Sports and Pastimes

1 What is the difference between a 'bosey' and a 'googly'?

2 Who was the Vice-Captain of the 'Rest of the World' cricket team in the (Test) matches against England in 1970?

3 On an English cricket score-card, byes, wides and no-balls are termed 'extras'. What are they called in Australia?

4 What is the basis on which counties are awarded bonus batting points in the English County Cricket Championship?

5 In a golf match, if your opponent gave you three strokes and a bisque, what would you do with the bisque?

6 Who plays what against whom for the Calcutta Cup?

7 What did Margaret Court do in 1970, which had been done only once before, in 1953?

8 And who performed a similar feat in 1953?

9 How many men are there in an American (Rugby) football team?

10 Who would do a double salchow and a double lutz?

11 How many players are there in a baseball team?

12 In boxing Ali beat Bonavene in which round?

Quiz One

Music

1 As whom was Bruno W. Schlesinger better known in the musical world?

2 Which famous musician's Christian names were Harold Malcolm Watts?

3 Who, what or where is, or was, Rudy Vallee?

4 Which American band leader and composer, famous for some forty to fifty years, bears the christian names Edward Kennedy?

5 Israel Baline was born in Russia in 1888. Subsequently he became one of the greatest song-writers of all time. As whom is he better known?

6 Musically speaking, as whom is Mrs Walter Legge better known?

7 The musical *Guys and Dolls* is based on characters created by whom?

8 Can you say who wrote an opera, first produced in 1945, based on Tolstoy's novel, *War and Peace*?

9 What is the name of Gilbert and Sullivan's 'Bunthorne's Bride'?

10 Who wrote the music to the ballet *Coppélia*?

11 Whereabouts would you expect to hear 'the intrusive h'?

12 Whose opera, *Falstaff*, was composed in his eightieth year?

Quiz One
General Knowledge

1 If you wanted to buy a spoon-back, where would you go, and why?

2 What does the following traffic sign denote: The black outlines of a motor-car under a motor-bike on a white background in a red circle?

3 Who is the Lady of the Thistle?

4 When is the Middle Watch at sea?

5 Trinity Term is a term at Oxford University. What else is it?

6 What is the title of the principal officer of a Fire Brigade in England?

7 What is the English translation of *Cavalleria Rusticana*?

8 In which country do 100 Filler equal 1 Forint?

9 Which county's inhabitants are nicknamed the 'Moon-rakers'?

10 What were the 'tares' mentioned in the parable of the tares, in St Matthew's gospel?

11 What did the swag-man carry in his tucker-bag?

12 Can you describe what a limber was (in the military sense of the word)?

Quiz Two

General Knowledge

1 What is the use of an inanimate painter?

2 The common sign of a pawnbroker – not so common in this more affluent day and age – was that of three golden balls. Can you say why?

3 What is the connection between an Asian herb, an open door and John Ruskin?

4 The capital of the Nord Department of France has given a word to the English language. Can you say what it is?

5 Can you say, to the nearest $\frac{1}{2}$ mph, what is the equivalent of 33 knots?

6 The number of Knights Companions of the Order of the Garter is limited. Can you say to how many?

7 What is the meaning of the abbreviation MVD to a Russian?

8 What is a Cheviot tup?

9 At what minimum age can an American become President?

10 And speaking about American Presidents, if none of the candidates has a majority, how is the President then elected?

11 According to Dr Johnson's celebrated remark, our forebears were highly unhygenic people and they carried a silver or golden ball containing aromatic substances, supposedly to ward off infection, but in fact, to alleviate their pungent BO. What were these gadgets called?

12 You may find a Mermaid's Purse on the sea-shore, those black rectangular things. What is a Mermaid's Purse?

Quiz Two

Words

1 Is a portress a coastal defence work, a small door in a nunnery, a cheap red wine, or what else is it?

2 Faro was a card game popular in France in the seventeenth century, in England in the eighteenth, and in the USA in the nineteenth. How did it get its name?

3 What does a speleologist study?

4 What was the function of a knapper?

5 What is the difference between a strath and a glen?

6 What is the difference between extrinsic and intrinsic?

7 What is the difference between agglomeration and conglomeration?

8 What is the difference between an isobar and an isotherm?

9 What does the verb 'to trammel' mean?

10 Where would you go if you wished to cantillate?

11 As what was the practice of buying and selling ecclesiastical benefices known?

12 We call it diaeresis; the Germans call it an umlaut. What do the French call it?

Quiz Two

Geography

1 In which country is Transylvania, if it exists at all?

2 What do Kermanshah, Hamadan, Mashed and Resht have in common?

3 Freeport is in the Bahamas. (There are also some Freeports in the USA.) Where is Freetown?

4 Which countries are separated by the Denmark Strait?

5 What is the geographical difference between Dinant and Dinan?

6 Except for about 50 miles of Atlantic coastline to the west, Gambia is entirely surrounded by another country. Can you identify the other country?

7 Of which South American state is New Amsterdam the second largest town?

8 Fredericton is the capital of which Canadian province?

9 What is the capital of North Korea?

10 The Mediterranean Sea is subdivided in places into five other seas. The Adriatic and the Aegean are two of them. Can you name one of the other three?

11 There are eight inhabited Hawaiian islands. Can you name one of them?

12 Of which country is Tegucigalpa the capital?

Quiz Two

History

1 What was Oliver Cromwell's real surname?

2 Where did William the Conqueror build an abbey to commemorate his victory at the Battle of Hastings in 1066?

3 Apart from Pym and Hampden, can you name one other of 'The Five Members' whom Charles I tried to arrest in 1642?

4 Whom did Perkin Warbeck claim to be, in his pretence to the throne of Henry VII?

5 What was the capital of the Jutish kings of Kent?

6 Which English king was murdered at Corfe Castle in Dorset, in 978?

7 William the Conqueror invaded England in 1066. Which other foreign ruler invaded the country in the same year?

8 Who was the mother of Queen Mary I of England?

9 Who was the father of King Henry VII?

10 Sir Francis Drake died in the West Indies in January 1596. Which other famous contemporary of Drake's died on the same expedition?

11 In whose reign did William Shakespeare die?

12 Which English king did Harold I of England succeed?

Quiz Two

People

1 Who was nicknamed 'Old Blood-and-Guts' in the Second World War?

2 What is the connection between George Psalmanazar and the island of Formosa?

3 George Galvin (1860–1904) was one of the best-loved stars of the English music-hall. What was his stage name?

4 What was the better-known name of the first Baron Tweedsmuir?

5 Which English author confessed to being an opium addict?

6 Who was the last Duke of York to ascend the throne of the United Kingdom?

7 Of which North American tribe was Sitting Bull the great warrior chief?

8 Who sang 'God Save the Emperor' when dying?

9 Lilian Alicia Marks made her name on the stage from 1924 until 1952. As whom was she better known?

10 What was the nationality of the author of *The Murders in the Rue Morgue*?

11 Under what other name do we know Mr Thomas Lanier Williams?

12 Can you name one of the three close relatives who are (at present) Field Marshals in the British Army?

Quiz Two

Literature

1 Shakespeare's Henry IV says, just before his death:
It hath been prophesied to me many years,
I should not die but in Jerusalem;
Did he? Explain the answer.

2 Who were Valentine and Proteus?

3 Apart from Oberon, Titania and Puck, there were four fairies in
Shakespeare's *A Midsummer Night's Dream*. Peaseblossom, Cobweb
and Mustardseed were three of them: who was the fourth?

4 Who was Olivia's steward in Shakespeare's *Twelfth Night*?

5 Which Shakespearian character said: 'Something is rotten in the state
of Denmark'?

6 Act III, Scene II of one of Shakespeare's plays opens with the
direction: 'Enter Shallow and Silence, meeting; Mouldy, Shadow,
Wart, Feeble, Bullcalf, and Servants, behind.' Can you identify the
play?

7 'Alas, poor Yorick! I knew him, Horatio, a fellow of infinite
jest. . . .' said Hamlet, when the gravediggers threw up the skull of the
former king's jester. Whose grave were they digging?

8 Shakespeare's Duke Senior in *As You Like It* considered the uses of
adversity to be sweet, in that it found: 'books in the running brooks,
and sermons in stones'. What did he say it found in the trees?

9 What was the name of the Vicar in *As You Like It*?

10 Who, in *Hamlet*, had 'A countenance more in sorrow than in anger'?

11 Into what did Hamlet wish that his 'too, too solid flesh would melt,
thaw, and resolve itself'?

12 Who, according to Shakespeare, was the son-in-law of Brabantio?

Quiz Two

Sports and Pastimes

1 Which football club first took the FA Cup out of England?

2 What are the colours of Welsh footballers at an international match?

3 Who, what or where is Wakefield Trinity?

4 What have Angels, Indians, Whitesox and Tigers in common?

5 In which country did dirt-track or speedway racing originate?

6 Are nursery cannons newly appointed prelates in a cathedral; a set of rules for very young children, small trench-mortars, or what else are they?

7 Who would take part in the '500'?

8 Who could tell the difference between a roller, a tippler and a tumbler?

9 Which game or sport is played in a pitch with forty-nine tolleys, where a fudge disqualifies the contestant, and the match is ended when the referee cries 'smug'?

10 How many balls are there on the billiard-table at the beginning of a frame of snooker?

11 W. G. Grace was one of the outstanding players in the history of cricket. What do the initials W. G. stand for?

12 How many dominoes are there in a set?

Quiz Two
Music

1 The player of a cembalo would now play which instrument?

2 Which normal orchestral instrument has the highest pitch?

3 Which note of the musical scale in any key is called the dominant?

4 Who was Lohengrin's father?

5 What is a musical 'accidental'?

6 Whereabouts in an orchestra would you find a homophone?

7 What does the musical direction, *sordini levati*, mean?

8 The famous aria *Una furtiva lagrima* has been sung by every great tenor for over a hundred years. What opera does it come from, or who composed it?

9 Musically speaking, why did A. C. Benson, Master of Eton (1885–1903) and Master of Magdalene College, Cambridge (1915–1925), who lived from 1862–1925, become famous?

10 What type of instrument is a pibroch?

11 The *theorbo* was much used in the seventeenth century. What was it?

12 What is a *berceuse*?

Quiz Two

General Knowledge

1 Which of the game birds turn all white during the winter?

2 Can you identify the extinct, flightless bird which was found only in New Zealand?

3 What method do the *vaqueros* use to catch ostriches in the Argentinian pampas?

4 In the UK, horses, cattle, sheep, goats and swine must be slaughtered if they have foot-and-mouth disease, or have been in immediate contact with it. On the Continent and in South America this is not so. Is this statement true or false, and can you explain your answer?

5 The capybara is an edible aquatic vegetarian mammal, related to the guinea-pig and resident in herds in the South American forests. What is peculiar about the capybara?

6 Which snake is alternatively known as the hamadryad?

7 Can you name the only fresh-water member of the cod family?

8 If you were given some ormers, what would you do with them?

9 Sepia is a fine brown pigment used in water-colour painting and in monochrome drawings. How was it originally obtained?

10 Which is the largest British fresh-water fish?

11 What kind of creature is a laverock?

12 Which is the second largest species of living bird?

Quiz Three

General Knowledge

1 Who solved the Riddle of the Sphinx of Thebes?

2 What was the Riddle of the Sphinx?

3 When is St David's Day?

4 Where and what is the Escorial?

5 What is the connection between a chopin and a mutchkin?

6 Why is a hearty eater termed a good trencherman?

7 Housewives see more and more metric descriptions on goods they buy in supermarkets. If it says, for instance, 1 kilogram on a packet of flour, how much would that be in pounds and ounces?

8 Churn drill – is it a special parade of Swiss dairy farmers at the annual fair at Aarau; is it a special treatment recommended by the Ministry of Agriculture, Fisheries and Food, for the sterilisation of milk churns; is it an old folk dance still surviving in County Kerry in Ireland, or what is it?

9 What is a jumper in mining?

10 Where would you expect to find a tylopod? And can you explain your answer?

11 Cattleyas, Odontoglossa and Cymbidia are all – what?

12 In the Beaufort Scale as what is Wind Force 11 known?

Quiz Three

Words

1 What is axolotl?

2 Would you say that an axometer is a person who measures the length of axolotls? Or what is an axometer?

3 If you were accused of mansuetude, would you be pleased or sorry? And why?

4 To pass muster now means to be accepted as adequate. What did the phrase originally mean?

5 What is a lapicide?

6 Can you describe what is meant by damascening?

7 Can you give an example of an umbriferous tree?

8 What is the chief characteristic of an aquiline nose?

9 What was the original meaning of the word 'tidy', now meaning neat and orderly?

10 Apart from its musical connotation, what is thrum?

11 According to the late Miss Dorothy Sayers, Lord Peter Wimsey wrote a book entitled *The Murderer's Vade-Mecum*. What is, or was, a vade-mecum?

12 Antonomasia is a figure of speech. Can you give an example of it?

Quiz Three
Geography

1 Which is the longest river in Europe?

2 Which is the longest mountain range in the world?

3 Which is Europe's largest inland port?

4 The North-west Passage is the name given to the route to China and the Orient round the north of the American continent. What is the North-east Passage?

5 What is the geographical name for 'The Spice Islands'?

6 Of which West African republic is Dakar the capital?

7 Missouri, Ohio, Minnesota, Illinois, Arkansas, Red, White and Yazo. What are they?

8 What is the name of the principal port on the delta of the River Volga?

9 Can you say whereabouts the River Rubicon is, or was?

10 In which country are the cities of Constantine, Oran, Annaba (formerly Bone), and Sidi-Bel-Abbes?

11 Which island, to the south-west of Majorca, is also a popular holiday resort?

12 Which is the largest lake in Europe?

Quiz Three

History

1 In which year did the Union of the Crowns of England and Scotland take place?

2 Which king surrendered his crown and kingdom into the hands of the Pope, and promised to rent them back for 1,000 marks per annum?

3 Can you say precisely where Admiral Lord Nelson was born on 29 September 1758?

4 Admiral Lord Nelson lost the sight of his right eye at the siege of Calvi in Corsica. Can you say at which engagement he lost his right leg?

5 Who or what are, or were, the Nonjurors?

6 Who built Caernarvon Castle?

7 Which English king was the son of Edward the Black Prince?

8 Who was the Sun-King of France?

9 Which king died in Pontefract Castle?

10 As whom was Richard of Bordeaux better known in England?

11 Who was the man nicknamed 'Henry Hotspur'?

12 Who or what were the 'Wobblies'?

Quiz Three
People

1 You have probably heard of the opera, *The Tales of Hoffman*. Who was Hoffman?

2 Which well-known poet and dramatist's christian names were Henrik Johan?

3 Van Gogh was one of the leaders of Post Impressionist painting. What was his christian name?

4 Which Austrian psychiatrist coined the term 'inferiority complex'?

5 Who was 'Artemus Ward'?

6 Eric Blair lived from 1903–50, and wrote a number of challenging best-sellers. As whom was he better known?

7 Which English poet married Anne Milbanke?

8 Who married Mary Powell in 1643, Catherine Woodcock in 1656 and Elizabeth Minshull in 1663?

9 In which year was Princess Anne born?

10 In which county was Sir Winston Churchill born?

11 Can you give the surnames of the brothers whose actual, though not professional, Christian names were Julius, Arthur, Leonard and Herbert?

12 Piggott once won the Grand National. Is this statement correct, and can you explain?

Quiz Three

Literature

1 Dumas Fils, the son of the author of *The Three Musketeers,* wrote a novel which was adapted as the libretto for Verdi's *La Traviata.* What was the name of the novel?

2 What did Homer call the city we call Troy?

3 What was the name of Sherlock Holmes's housekeeper?

4 Which British novelist wrote *Northanger Abbey*?

5 *The Forsyte Saga* is to John Galsworthy as what is to Hugh Walpole?

6 Which famous author's first published novel was entitled *A Dinner at Poplar,* or *Mr Minns and His Cousin*?

7 *Combe and tor, green meadow and lane,*
Birds on the waving bough;
Beetling cliffs by the surging main;
Rich red loam for the plough.
What is Sir Harold Boulton describing?

8 Who wrote *The Second Mrs Tanqueray*?

9 What was Scrooge's Christian name?

10 Who, in his *Faerie Queene*, named whom Gloriana?

11 David Belasco (1853–1931) was a well-known American dramatist, theatre manager and trainer of players, after whom a New York theatre was named. What was his connection, if any, with Puccini?

12 Can you name the British playwright who wrote the two very successful plays, *The Winslow Boy* and *French Without Tears*?

Quiz Three

Sports and Pastimes

1 How many players are there in a water polo team?

2 Which Football League club's home ground is known as Turf Moor?

3 'The Den' is the home ground of which football club?

4 Who were the English Football League Champions in 1969/70?

5 What have Accrington Stanley, Gateshead and New Brighton in common?

6 In boxing, the maximum weight for a flyweight is 112 lb. The maximum weight for a bantamweight is 118 lb. What is the maximum weight for a heavyweight?

7 What is the definition of the word 'dormy' as used in the game of golf?

8 How did the 'little man from Rockhampton' achieve fame in June 1968?

9 What is the longest athletic event in the Olympic Games?

10 Which British football ground holds the record for paying spectators at a match?

11 In which world championship have the finals frequently been played by the Toucon Terribles from Tinsley Green and the Johnson Jets from Langley Green?

12 What was the name of the famous product of Archive and Bright Cherry?

Quiz Three
Music

1 Christian Sinding composed two violin concertos, a piano concerto, chamber music and more than two hundred songs. But about the only composition for which he is remembered in this country is an early piano piece, *Rustle of Spring*. What was Sinding's nationality?

2 What was the traditional tune twice mentioned by Shakespeare in *The Merry Wives of Windsor* (1602) and by other writers of this period? It is first referred to in the Stationer's Company Register as 'a new Northern Dittye', in 1580, but it is thought to be older. Pepys alludes to it, and Vaughan Williams composed an orchestral fantasia on it.

3 Who wrote *The Lark Quartet*?

4 Who wrote the music to the opera *Simone Boccanegra*?

5 For which monarch is Handel thought to have written his instrumental suite called the *Water Music*?

6 Who wrote the music to the operas *The Sorcerer* and *The Grand Duke*?

7 Of which opera is Captain Macheath the hero?

8 Can you name one of the two operas written by Michael Ivanovitch Glinka?

9 Who wrote the incidental music to Ibsen's *Peer Gynt*?

10 The composer of *The Rite of Spring* died on 6 April 1971. Who was he?

11 If grelots are used in an orchestra, how are they used?

12 Which steel percussion instrument is named from its shape?

Quiz Three
General Knowledge

1 The abbreviation BSA calls to mind today a famous motor-cycle. Can you say what the initials stand for?

2 What is the connection between a gymkhana and a rackets court?

3 There is a succession of reservoirs in the beautiful Elan Valley, south-west of Rhayader in Radnorshire. Which city do they serve?

4 Under what circumstances would a Roman have called his boss an 'umbo'?

5 What, precisely, is the Privy Purse?

6 Did the Truck System have anything to do with transport? If not, what did it have to do with?

7 The old twelve-sided threepenny piece was officially described as being composed of 'Nickel Brass', commonly called by the banks 'Nickel'. Can you say, to within 5 per cent, how much nickel there was in it?

8 What does a squaloid creature look like?

9 A slype is a Northern Irish dialect term for the yellow-banded earthworm. Right or wrong, and explain your answer.

10 What is the name of the first ocean-going screw steamer designed by Brunel in 1845, and recently brought back from the Falkland Islands to undergo a two-year renovation in Bristol?

11 Which expression, commonly used of one suspected of being a traitor in the Second World War, was said to have been coined by General Mola in the Spanish Civil War?

12 What do the Germans call what the French call 'Mont Cervin'?

Quiz Four

General Knowledge

1 A Dogberry is an officious and ignorant Jack-in-the-office. Where did the name originate?

2 The Vatican has suggested that certain pieces of profane music should not be played in Catholic churches. Among them is Mendelssohn's *Wedding March*. What was the reason given why this popular music should no longer be played?

3 The Romans called it *Lindum*. What do we call it?

4 What was the 'Godless Florin'?

5 Which Second World War aircraft was nicknamed 'Stringbag'?

6 What are the most common sources of tannin, or tannic acid?

7 Whose dying words were these: 'All my possessions for a moment of time'?

8 The present capital of the Isle of Man is Douglas. What was the ancient capital?

9 Where is the Richmondshire Festival held?

10 The Trappists are an Order of monks who have taken the vow of silence. Why are the Trappists so called?

11 In the seventeenth century a Calcutta punch, a London punch and a Devon punch were similar in that they were composed of the same five principal ingredients: a spirit, water, spice, sugar and lemon juice. A Suffolk punch was essentially different. Can you say how?

12 What is a craneway?

Quiz Four

Words

1 In the first Queen Elizabeth's time, a common form of curse was: 'A murrain on thee!' What precisely was murrain?

2 Why is crêpe rubber so called?

3 What is a 'unicameral legislature'?

4 What was the original meaning of 'to take umbrage'?

5 What, precisely, is a polyglot?

6 What is the study of handwriting called?

7 To a yachtsman, what is a grommet (or grummet)?

8 What would you do with a cataplasm?

9 If you were given a peruke, what would you do with it?

10 What is the right of piscary?

11 Would you be pleased or sorry if your wife told you she had a sorosis? And why?

12 Can you give the precise meaning of the verb to evanesce?

Quiz Four

Geography

1 If you travel from Edinburgh on the A9 to its terminal, where would you end up?

2 Which northern cathedral city stands on the River Ure?

3 Can you name one of the three counties of Eire which are in the Province of Ulster?

4 In which county does the River Trent rise?

5 Which river runs into the sea at Littlehampton?

6 Can you say, to within five miles, the farthest you can get from the seas in England?

7 Man and his man – what are they?

8 Of which county is Castlebar the county town?

9 The Scots will probably never forgive the English for Culloden. In which county is Culloden?

10 Kingston in Ireland is now called – what?

11 In which Irish county is Tiree?

12 In which county is the capital city of Eire?

Quiz Four

History

1 In AD 150 London had the largest known Basilica, outside Rome. Do you know where it was located?

2 The Fire of London in 1666 destroyed 13,200 houses and St Paul's Cathedral and 89 churches. How many people were killed?

3 As what is the fifteenth-century village of Tyburn now known?

4 Can you say, to within a hundred years, when the figure of Britannia first appeared on a coin of this realm?

5 Whereabouts in London, in the seventeenth century, was Alsatia?

6 In Jonathan's Coffee House in the City of London they obviously drank coffee, but in 1698 they added to their activities – in what way?

7 In which English counties were the termini of the ancient Icknield Way?

8 Which part of the British Isles did the Romans know as Mona?

9 There is a village in Kent called Horsted, between Maidstone and Chatham. Why is it of historical interest?

10 By the order of which monarch was Ascot racecourse laid out?

11 To which of the Hebrides did Bonnie Prince Charlie flee, after Culloden, on his way to France?

12 Can you name the clan, over thirty members of which, as well as the chief, were massacred at Glencoe in 1692?

Quiz Four

People

1 Which famous actress played the part of Hamlet after she had lost a leg?

2 What was the nationality of the late Kirsten Flagstad, the famous Wagnerian opera singer?

3 Which famous dancer and choreographer shared his name with the 1970 Derby winner?

4 Who coined the immortal phrase: 'include me out'?

5 What is the name of the Sherpa who accompanied Sir Edmund Hillary to the summit of Mount Everest in 1953?

6 What royal appointment did Sir Walford Davies hold from 1934–1941?

7 As whom was Alexandra Fydorovna better known?

8 What was Tchaikovsky's first name?

9 What is the family name of the Duke of Marlborough?

10 What relation is the Duke of Rothesay to the Duke of Edinburgh?

11 What was Louis Stephen St Laurent's claim to fame?

12 Can you name a famous cousin of Rudyard Kipling?

Quiz Four

Literature

1 Who lived in 'Doubting Castle'?

2 Uncle Remus used to tell stories about Brer Rabbit and Brer Fox. Who created Uncle Remus?

3 Sergeanne Golon created which well-known character of fiction?

4 Who invented the character of Pantagruel?

5 Which Scottish novelist was responsible for *The Admirable Crichton*?

6 According to the nursery rhyme, why did the King of Spain's daughter come to visit me?

7 According to Edward Lear's Book of Nonsense:
There was a young lady of Wilts,
Who walked up to Scotland on stilts;
When they said it was shocking
To show so much stocking,
She answered . . . ?
What *did* she answer?

8 Can you say who wrote the following?
A lifetime of happiness! No man alive could bear it; it would be hell on earth.

9 Who, according to John Keats, stood, *Silent upon a peak in Darien*?

10 In which work do the lines in question 9 appear?

11 Can you identify the Victorian author who wrote: *The Ordeal of Richard Feverel*; *Rhoda Fleming*; *The Adventures of Harry Richmond* and *Diana of the Crossways*?

12 According to Dr Johnson, who 'touched nothing that he did not adorn'?

Quiz Four

Sports and Pastimes

1 Where were the Olympic Games held in 1936, the last Games before the war?

2 Who was nicknamed the 'Brown Bomber'?

3 Who competes at what for the Dewar Cup?

4 What is the correct diameter of each hole on a golf-course?

5 What sport is held at Altcar, near Liverpool, for three days during February each year?

6 How many players were capped more than a hundred times for playing in England's soccer team?

7 In cricket, what is a leg bye?

8 For what sport was George Herman Ruth famous, and what was he more usually known as?

9 In which town does the Scottish football club 'Queen of the South' have its ground?

10 Which Scottish football team is popularly known as 'The Hi Hi', and also by another nickname: 'The Warriors'?

11 In which indoor sport could you observe the balk line?

12 How many players are there in a Rugby Union side and a Rugby League side?

Quiz Four
Music

1 For which occasion was *Land of Hope and Glory* written?

2 Who composed the famous *Valse Triste* in the incidental music to the drama *Kuolema*?

3 What does the musical direction *con sordino* mean?

4 What was a *rebec(k)* or *ribible*?

5 In which German town are the annual Wagner Festivals held?

6 *Mezzo* combined with other words is a common musical expression. What, literally, does *mezzo* mean?

7 The Germans and the Americans describe their musical notes as whole-notes, and fractions of notes, down to a sixty-fourth note. What do we call what they call a whole-note?

8 What do we call the musical note the French call a *croche*, or *crochet*?

9 Which famous ballet has the sub-title *The Girl with the Enamelled Eyes*?

10 Which twentieth-century composer wrote the music of the opera-oratorio *Oedipus Rex*?

11 Who composed the opera, or rather masque, called *Semele*?

12 What is the alternative, and better-known title of Mozart's opera *Il Dissoluto Punito* (The Rake Punished)?

Quiz Four

General Knowledge

1 There is a Naked Boy Court and a Naked Boy Alley in London. Why are they so called?

2 Every state of the USA has an official state flower. Of which state is the magnolia the official flower?

3 What exactly is curd?

4 Which figures appear on the badge of the Order of the Garter?

5 What is the difference in shape between macaroni and fettucini?

6 Capers are often used in salads, sauces, etc. What are they?

7 Angelica – the type that is used in cooking – comes from the angelica plant. What part of the plant?

8 What is the principal source of Vitamin C?

9 What is the seed-bud of a potato called?

10 After how many years' marriage do you celebrate your Pearl Wedding?

11 What would an ancient Scot have done in his Broch?

12 What is the standard gauge of railway track in this country?

Quiz Five

General Knowledge

1 Which creature is colloquially known as the 'butterbump'?

2 What do the Jugoslavs do in the Skupshtina?

3 Whereabouts in the human body is the sternum?

4 What kind of creature is a tittle-bat?

5 Where was the earliest English fine porcelain made?

6 What is the more popular name for the Jamaica pepper?

7 What is the Court of Arches?

8 What does the expression 'A Roland for an Oliver' mean?

9 And how did this expression arise?

10 What is the more common name of the ember goose?

11 What are the termini of the fastest railway train in the world?

12 What was a brattice-cloth to a coal miner?

Quiz Five

Words

1 To whom would who be a Gorgio (or Gorgie)?

2 Where would you be likely to find scobs?

3 What is the difference between eruption and irruption?

4 What is a sprit?

5 And what is a spruit in South Africa?

6 *Paleo* – as in paleolithic, paleobotany, etc. What does *paleo* mean?

7 What is the pangolin?

8 What, precisely, is an integer?

9 What is a polony?

10 If you had eupepsia, would you be pleased or sorry, and why?

11 Is a charpoy a tea-pot, a waiter in an Indian tea-shop, a tea-planter in Assam, the son of a charwoman, or what else is he or it?

12 What is a postulant?

Quiz Five

Geography

1 On which river is Calcutta situated?

2 What is Texarkana?

3 If the Cantabrian Mountains are not in Cambridgeshire, where are they?

4 Which is the largest of the United States of America, in area?

5 Which is the largest city and capital of the North Italian region of Piedmont?

6 Between which two countries does the River Zambesi form the frontier?

7 Which is the twin city of Khartoum, on the opposite side of the White Nile?

8 What is the capital of Malawi?

9 In which Asian country are the Taurus Mountains?

10 Which group of Greek islands includes Andros, Tenos, Naxos, Melos and Paros?

11 Which is the northernmost department of France?

12 Which two West Indian countries are separated by the Windward Passage?

Quiz Five

History

1 The Pilgrim Fathers set sail from Southampton on 5 August 1620, in two ships, but had to put in to Dartmouth when one of them was found to be in need of repair. A second start was made from Monkey Quay, Dartmouth, but bad weather drove them into Plymouth Sound, where the unseaworthy ship was abandoned. What was its name?

2 Washington became America's capital in 1800. What was the capital of the United States before that?

3 Which was the first English colony in America?

4 Can you say, to within ten years, when the Dominion of Canada came into being?

5 Which state of the USA is nicknamed 'The first State' and claims to be the first of the original thirteen States to be admitted to the Union?

6 Who was the only United States President elected for four consecutive terms of office?

7 Four US Presidents have been assassinated whilst in office. One British Prime Minister has suffered the same fate. Can you identify him?

8 Which was the last English territorial possession in France to be lost?

9 Which was the last of the British Crown Colonies to obtain its independence, in October 1970?

10 After whose Queen was the capital of South Australia named?

11 After whom are the Goodwin Sands, off the East Coast of Kent, named?

12 New York was named after which king of Great Britain?

Quiz Five

People

1 Has Giacomo Agostini yet held an exhibition of his paintings in London. If so, where? If not, why not?

2 Who married Lady Alice Montagu-Douglas-Scott in 1935?

3 How old was William Shakespeare when he died?

4 As whom is Bernard Marmaduke Fitzalan-Howard better known?

5 She lived from 1874–1937; she was niece of Emma Cons, who took over the Music Hall known as the Royal Victoria Hall in 1880. She was well-known as a child violinist and afterwards as a concert entertainer. She, herself, took over the management of the Royal Victoria Hall – which became the Old Vic – in 1898, after which it became the home of Shakespearian drama and of opera. Who was she?

6 Which famous film star won an Oscar for his portrayal of a Roman Catholic priest in the film called *Going My Way*?

7 Archibald Leach was born in Bristol in 1904, emigrated to the USA in 1921 and by the late 1930s had established himself as one of the best light-comedy film actors. What is his stage name?

8 Who was the original 'It' girl of the film world? 'It' being translated as 'sex appeal'.

9 Which American actress and singer made her name in the film *The Wizard of Oz*?

10 Herbert Frahm was born in Lübeck in 1913. He worked in the anti-Nazi underground movement in Germany under an assumed name, and spent twelve years in exile in Scandinavia. He is now world-famous under that assumed name. Who is he?

11 Under which name did the writer Korzeniovsky become famous as a novelist?

12 Which famous British soldier was known as 'K of K'?

Quiz Five

Literature

1 What is the sequel to Anthony Hope's famous novel, *The Prisoner of Zenda*?

2 In which country are Anthony Hope's two novels set?

3 Can you quote the line preceding:
In the spring a young man's fancy lightly turns to thoughts of love,
from Tennyson's *Locksley Hall*?

4 Where would you find the three brothers, Sansfoy, Sansjoy and Sansloy?

5 Lady Castlewood is a character in which famous novel?

6 Where, according to Tennyson, did Sir Richard Grenville lay?

7 What was he doing there?

8 By which work is Sir Thomas Malory remembered?

9 Who wrote a poem in memory of his great friend, Arthur Henry Hallam?

10 *Adonais*, by Percy Bysshe Shelley, was an elegy on the death of a friend. Can you say who the friend was?

11 What was the occupation of Thomas Gradgrind in Dickens's *Hard Times*?

12 Which Anglo-American author wrote *The Turn of the Screw* and *The Wings of a Dove* around the turn of the century?

Quiz Five

Sports and Pastimes

1 Which football team is known as 'The Canaries'?

2 West Indian cricket, in the 1950s, was dominated by three great batsmen nicknamed the 'Three Ws'. Can you name them?

3 On which racecourse is the Cesarewitch Handicap run?

4 The Oxford–Cambridge boat race in 1912 caused a tremendous sensation. Why?

5 If a Scotsman 'burned the water', what would he be doing?

6 Who plays what at Sabina Park, Kingston, Jamaica?

7 Who plays what for the Sheffield Shield?

8 In which game do you have bamboos, circles, characters, honours and winds?

9 What game, played with a stick and a ball, is said to have originated with the North American Indians?

10 Which is the oldest rowing race still rowed in England?

11 Which body made the rules for lawn tennis as played today?

12 What have Arosa, Chamonix and Lillehammer in common?

Quiz Five
Music

1 What is the connection between the son of Cush and Sir Edward Elgar?

2 Paul Tortellier had orchestral experience with the Paris Conservatoire Orchestra and the Boston Symphony, since when he has become a world-famous soloist. On which instrument?

3 Who wrote the music to the opera entitled *The Turn of the Screw*? To give you a hint as to the period, the libretto was based on a story by Henry James.

4 Victorien Sardou wrote a play upon which Puccini based an opera. Can you say which one?

5 What did Chopin call what Beethoven called a *Nachtstück*?

6 What is the popular name for the Symphony No. 8 in D minor by Schubert?

7 In which country did Beethoven first hear his Ninth Symphony performed?

8 How many piano sonatas did Beethoven write?

9 How many symphonies did Haydn write?

10 *Les Six* were a group of French composers, formed in Paris in 1917 to further the interests of modern music. Can you name one of them?

11 Who would be likely to adopt the practice of 'flutter-tonguing'?

12 Who is the composer, lyricist and playwright famous for his successful musical *Oliver*?

Quiz Five

General Knowledge

1 Alexander Nevski was a famous thirteenth-century Russian warrior-hero and saint. The principal thoroughfare in one of the world's best-planned and beautiful cities is named after him. Can you identify the city?

2 After which territory was New Zealand named?

3 What does a diesinker do?

4 How many annas are there to a rupee in India?

5 The longest period during which Bank Rate in this country has remained unchanged was the twelve years from 1939–51. Can you say what the rate was, during that period?

6 The golden guinea was first introduced by Charles II in 1663. What was its nominal value then?

7 As what is the 'leontopodium alpinum' better known? The clue is in the name.

8 What is the colour of the flower of the celandine?

9 Which flower is the Imperial flower of Japan?

10 What is the 'Poor Man's Weatherglass'?

11 And which flower means, translated, the rose-tree?

12 Who or what is known as 'The King of the Waters'?

Quiz Six

General Knowledge

1 The man who invented the bifurcated dagger invented the first – what?

2 Whereabouts in England is Scotland?

3 Until 1824 it was called Plymouth Dock – what was it called after that?

4 Who played the part of Henry Higgins in the first film of Bernard Shaw's *Pygmalion*?

5 Which metal is extracted from bauxite?

6 Where is the Parliamentary division of Sutton?

7 What is the incorrect similarity between the River Avon and Lake Nyasa?

8 And as what is Lake Nyasa known today?

9 If you were physically capable of it, when and how would you perform an entrechat?

10 How many times a year do peacocks lay their eggs?

11 'The oak is one of the very few trees outside South America which has two different fruits; the acorn and the oak-apple.' True or false? And explain your answer.

12 What is the precise function of an eccentric gear?

Quiz Six

Words

1 Who would have sent what through a balistraria in the Middle Ages?

2 What were arbalesters?

3 What, precisely, is a synod?

4 What is the difference between a paragon and a paradigm?

5 A pseudonym is a nom-de-plume; a pseudoscope is an optical instrument which makes convex objects seem concave and vice versa. If someone described you as a pseudologer, would you be pleased or sorry? And why?

6 Pidgin English is, as you know, a corrupted form of English used widely in the East, but do you know what the word 'Pidgin' means?

7 You probably know what a lych-gate is. What is, or was, the lych, from which it took its name?

8 What is the meaning of the word, licit?

9 What is longanimity?

10 Georg Ohm (1787–1854) was a famous German physicist. Was he also an eponym? If not, why not?

11 What, precisely, is a tintinnabulation?

12 A southpaw today commonly applies to a boxer who adopts a stance with the right hand and foot forward; the opposite of the traditional method. What, originally, in America, was a southpaw?

Quiz Six

Geography

1 Is the name 'Gulf Stream' a misnomer, or does it really emanate from a gulf? If so, which one?

2 What, who, or where are Mauna Kea and Mauna Loa?

3 Italy is on one side of the Strait of Otranto; what is on the other?

4 In Plantagenet times the ancient French Provinces of Maine, Touraine and Aquitaine belonged to England. Can you say where Aquitaine was?

5 Can you name one of the rivers which form the border between Poland and East Germany?

6 Only two rivers form part of the frontier between Canada and the USA. The St Lawrence is one; which is the other?

7 The better known Frankfurt is in West Germany, twenty-five miles east of Wiesbaden. On which river is this Frankfurt situated?

8 The Netherlands Antilles comprise three islands off the north coast of Venezuela, and three more some 500 miles to the north-east. Can you name one of these islands?

9 The Victoria Falls, with a drop of about 400 feet, present one of the most beautiful sights in the African continent. On which river do they occur?

10 Who, what or where is, or was, the Great Karroo?

11 What is the capital of Zambia?

12 Which territories are separated by the Cook Strait?

Quiz Six

History

1 Who succeeded Priam as King of Troy?

2 'One of Emperor Nero's greatest delights was to watch the Gladiatorial contests in the Colosseum. It is, however, wrong to say that he played the fiddle while Rome burned, because at that time the fiddle hadn't been invented.' What is wrong with that statement?

3 Over which people did 'The Scourge of God' reign from AD 434 to 453?

4 After the death of Julius Caesar, Rome was ruled by a Triumvirate of Mark Antony, Lepidus and Octavian. This broke up in 31 BC and Octavian ruled Rome until 27 BC. From 27 BC until AD 14 Augustus was Emperor. What was the relationship between Octavian and Augustus?

5 In medieval times, the country now known as Albania was called Illyria or Illyricum. What part of the world was then known as Albania?

6 Whereabouts did the Minoan civilisation thrive?

7 What was the capital city of Ancient Assyria?

8 Can you name the ruler who suspended, by a single horse-hair, the sword over the head of Damocles?

9 Who was the first wife of Alexander the Great?

10 Which school of ancient Greek philosophy was founded by Antisthenes about 400 BC, and later led by Diogenes?

11 How and where did Mark Antony meet his death?

12 The Romans called it *Aquae Sulis*. What do we call it?

Quiz Six

People

1 Who were called 'The White Friars'?

2 Who was called 'The Red Dean' of Canterbury?

3 Glamis Castle, in Angus, Scotland, was the childhood home of the Lady Elizabeth Bowes-Lyon, daughter of the Earl of Strathmore and Kinghorne. As whom is she known today?

4 Joseph Priestley (1733–1804), the discoverer of oxygen, was by profession, what?

5 Who leads the band that calls itself 'The Knock-outs'?

6 He was the illegitimate son of an actress, who placed him with a Billingsgate fish-porter. He was a newsboy in Deptford; spent seven years in the army; became a War Correspondent from 1899 to 1902, and published his first full-length novel in 1905. From then on he built up a reputation as the leading crime thriller writer in Europe if not in the world. Who was he?

7 W. H. Auden is a famous Anglo-American poet. Can you give one of his Christian names?

8 What association was formed by the two well-known novelists, Pamela Hansford Johnson and C. P. Snow (now Lord Snow), in 1950?

9 What have the following in common: Gordon Cooper, Thomas Stafford, Michael Collins and Richard Gordon?

10 In 1843 Sir Henry Cole received something from his friend J. C. Horsley which is regarded as the first of its kind. What was it?

11 The monk Dom Perignon is traditionally credited with the invention of what?

12 For what were Marie Camargo and Fanny Elssler famous?

Quiz Six

Literature

1 In which country did Shakespeare set *A Midsummer Night's Dream*?

2 According to Shakespeare, who was Prospero's daughter?

3 *My father named me . . .; who being, as I am, littered under Mercury, was likewise a snapper-up of unconsidered trifles.*
According to Shakespeare, what had his father named him?

4 In *A Midsummer Night's Dream* Bottom was a weaver and Snug was a joiner. What craft was practised by Quince?

5 According to Shakespeare, who was the son of Sycorox, the witch?

6 In Shakespeare's *King Henry VI, Part III,* Richard, Duke of Gloucester, afterwards King Richard III, comments:
Why, what a peevish fool was that of Crete
That taught his son the office of a fowl!
And yet, for all his wings, the fool was drowned.
Who was the 'peevish fool' of Crete?

7 What was Prospero's title?

8 Why is Shakespeare's *Twelfth Night* so called?

9 In which of Shakespeare's historical plays do Ralph Mouldy, Simon Shadow and Francis Feeble appear?

10 In the cast of the same play, Shakespeare lists five other characters as 'Irregular Humourists'. Can you name one of them?

11 Over which country did King Lear rule?

12 In which of Shakespeare's plays do the Count and Countess of Rousillon, the King of France, the Duke of Florence, and Lavache, a clown, appear?

Quiz Six
Sports and Pastimes

1 In which field did V. T. Trumper become famous?

2 Where do the following events take place: the Grand Challenge Cup, the Ladies Challenge Plate, the Stewards Challenge Cup and the Visitors Challenge Cup?

3 For what are the Harlem Globetrotters famous?

4 If you were in a field with a plate and a pitcher and you weren't having a picnic, what would you be doing?

5 How many pockets are there on an American billiard table?

6 In which sport would you be taking part if you heard the words dojo, o-soto-gari and randori?

7 Only one bowler in the history of cricket has taken over three hundred wickets in Test matches. Can you name him?

8 What is the length of a cricket pitch?

9 Who was the first person to swim the English Channel?

10 If a golfer speaks of the 'Colonel', what does he mean?

11 Can you describe the game of knur and spell, and name one of the three implements needed to play it?

12 On what sporting instrument would you find a button, a foible, a forte and a cushion?

Quiz Six
Music

1 Who was the earliest of the following six composers: Beethoven, Mendelssohn, Handel, Mozart, Schubert and Haydn?

2 Gilbert and Sullivan wrote *The Sorcerer*. Who wrote *The Sorcerer's Apprentice*?

3 What is a mediant?

4 Which note of the musical scale is called by the Germans 'H'?

5 What is the alternative title of Gilbert and Sullivan's *HMS Pinafore*?

6 Leonora, Florestan, Rocco and Pizarro are characters in which famous opera?

7 Who composed the *Jupiter* Symphony?

8 What is the name of the Lord High Executioner in *The Mikado*?

9 In which opera does 'Mrs Ellen Orford' appear?

10 Which was the last opera composed by Wagner?

11 In which of Handel's works would you hear *The Hailstone Chorus*?

12 Who composed the Scotch Symphony and the Italian Symphony?

Quiz Six
General Knowledge

1 Whereabouts is the famous *Shwe Dagon* pagoda, which is plated with pure gold?

2 What is, or was, a joss-house?

3 Who is the patron saint of shoemakers, whose feast day is 25 October?

4 Which creature, real or imaginary, is represented by Capricorn, the tenth sign of the zodiac?

5 What is the second sign of the zodiac?

6 Which commercially named bird is also known as the serpent-eater?

7 What are logan stones?

8 Alexander Selkirk was marooned by Dampier on the island of Fernando Po in 1709, where he remained until rescued in 1714. The episode gave Defoe the idea for his *Robinson Crusoe*. True or false? And why?

9 What do the initials B.S.M. stand for in the British Army?

10 As whom is Jack Dawkins better known to Dickensian addicts?

11 What is the *Kalevala*?

12 In which city was 'Expo '70' held?

Quiz Seven

General Knowledge

1 Where would you find a falx?

2 What is a harvestman?

3 What is the connection between frog-hoppers and cuckoo-spit?

4 What is the colloquial name for the cockchafer?

5 Is an Alpine Accentor a mountain railway, a ski-lift, a mountain guide, a Swiss interpreter, a rocky cleft which causes a peculiar echo? Or what else is it?

6 Three 'A's, two 'R's, a 'D', 'K' and 'V'. Put them together and they spell the name of an animal? Which?

7 Which is the odd one out of the following: pine marten, house martin, stoat, weasel, polecat and mink?

8 What kind of creature is an *ursine colobus*?

9 Who or what was Landseer's 'Monarch of the Glen'?

10 What do the Palouse, Minnesota No. 2 and Poland China have in common?

11 What is the correct term for the tail of an otter?

12 What is the correct name for a young peacock?

Quiz Seven

Words

1 What are exequies?

2 If a grammalogue is not an old peasant woman collecting kindling in the forest, what else is it?

3 What is another name for variola?

4 If you were an orthoëpist, what would you be particularly careful about?

5 Is a fumitory a railway smoking carriage, an anti-smog device, an oriental dope-den, an air-vent in a brewery? Or what is it?

6 What is the correct word to describe the colour and appearance of unbleached linen? It comes direct from the French.

7 What is the modern equivalent of the Latin phrase: *nolens volens*?

8 'A good chap' now denotes a good friend, or a good fellow. Can you say why 'chap'?

9 If you were to make a political broadcast, and you were introduced by the announcer as the 'nescient' Member of Parliament for Seatown, would you be pleased, sorry, embarrassed, or what? And why?

10 What is an immiscible substance?

11 If you became pedicular, would you be pleased or sorry?

12 If you indulged in oscitation during a medical lecture, would your lecturer be pleased or sorry? And why?

Quiz Seven
Geography

1 Which river runs under the famous Clifton Suspension Bridge?

2 Which river runs through Newport, Monmouthshire and into the Severn about four miles to the south?

3 What is the county town of the Scottish county of Moray?

4 Which city in the United Kingdom is served by Aldergrove airport?

5 What is 'Peckham Rye' used for?

6 Of which territory is Thorshavn the capital?

7 Can you name the island almost exactly halfway between the Orkneys and the Shetlands?

8 In which English county is Philadelphia?

9 Yorkshire is the largest county in England; which is the second largest?

10 Which river was the boundary between the old English kingdoms of Mercia and Northumbria?

11 And which counties does it separate now?

12 Which is the largest tract of land in the Firth of Clyde?

Quiz Seven

History

1 Who was the first Czar of Russia?

2 Who was the first woman to be elected a Member of the House of Commons?

3 Which English king was, according to tradition, murdered in the Tower of London by Richard III?

4 Which English king married Catherine of Valois?

5 The mother of King Henry VI, the last Lancastrian king, was also the grandmother of King Henry VII, the first of the Tudors. Can you explain?

6 Henry Chichele was Archbishop of Canterbury from 1414–43, and founded a unique college at Oxford in 1437. Which Oxford college was it, and why is it unique?

7 Frederick Barbarossa was crowned Holy Roman Emperor by an Englishman. Do you know the Englishman's name, or his title?

8 Who began the building of the Tower of London?

9 In whose reign was the title of baronet introduced?

10 What was the title of Simon de Montfort?

11 Which British Crown Dependency calls itself *Ellan Vannin*?

12 What was Lord Nelson's naval rank when he died at Trafalgar?

Quiz Seven

People

1 Who were the three stars of the radio show 'Much Binding in the Marsh'?

2 Whose favourite wife was Ayesha?

3 Who was the mother of King Solomon?

4 Which king was entranced by the dancing of Salome?

5 Whom did the nineteenth-century Polynesians entitle 'Tusitala', 'The Teller of Tales'?

6 In spite of the fact that examples of their work must have been seen by about 90 per cent of the population of the UK, the names of the artists Mr Arnold Machin, RA, and Mr Christopher Ironside are not very widely known in this country. Whereabouts would you think you have seen their work?

7 What have Percy Spencer Beale, Leslie Kenneth O'Brien and John Standish Fforde in common?

8 After which English king is the Scottish capital named?

9 Miss Harriet Wilson blackmailed her lovers by threatening to expose them in her memoirs – among them was the Duke of Wellington. What is he reported to have said?

10 James McGill was born in Glasgow in 1744, emigrated to Canada, and made a fortune out of fur trading. For what is he principally remembered?

11 Who is the Master of the Merchant Navy and Fishing Fleets?

12 And who is the Master of the Corporation of Trinity House?

Quiz Seven

Literature

1 Who used the first words of Virgil's *Aeneid* as the title of a play?

2 Who was the unlikely author of:
   What of the bow?
   The bow was made in England;
   Of true wood, of yew wood,
   The wood of English bows?

3 Who wrote *The Swiss Family Robinson*, slightly plagiaristic of Defoe's *Robinson Crusoe*, but very popular in Europe during the nineteenth century?

4 Which famous nineteenth-century author recalled his own prison experiences in a novel called *The House of the Dead*?

5 Which famous British author of detective stories created the tough characters, Slim Callaghan, the detective, and his assistant, Lemmy Caution?

6 Who wrote the novels *The Black Tulip* and *The Corsican Brothers*?

7 Which famous author and poet lived at Abbotsford?

8 What was the title of the best-selling novel written by Anita Loos and published in 1925?

9 Which English poet and author received a Nobel Prize, and three times declined the honour of the Order of Merit?

10 Who was the author of *Dr Jekyll and Mr Hyde*?

11 What had Marion Sharpe and her mother to do with the end of a certain 'Franchise'?

12 In his translation of *Don Quixote*, Smollett gave a name to Sancho Panza's horse, which Cervantes had left anonymous. What name did Smollett invent?

Quiz Seven

Sports and Pastimes

1 Which is the highest hand at Poker (excluding the use of jokers and 'wild' cards)?

2 What is the literal meaning of the expression 'checkmate' in the game of chess?

3 A gambit is now a tricky move in many games. Originally it was an opening in chess. What does a chess gambit entail?

4 What does the term *passe* mean at roulette?

5 If you were experienced in Kendo, what implements would you use for it?

6 If you were experienced in Aikido on what occasion would this knowledge come in very useful?

7 An Order of General Monk, in 1662, stated: 'No persons shall after play carry their malls out of St James's Parke without leave of the keeper'. Can you explain this? What are the 'malls'?

8 What is a 'bird' in Badminton?

9 And how did the game of Badminton get its name?

10 At which game do you have a point, cover point, third man and a goalkeeper?

11 How many pieces are there in a full mah-jong set?

12 What were the rules of the game of pitch and toss?

Quiz Seven

Music

1 From which musical show does the famous song *Tea for Two* come?

2 If Cardinal Newman's *Dream of Gerontius* had not been beautifully set to music, it would probably not be nearly so well known as it is today. Who was responsible for the musical setting?

3 What was the signature tune of the BBC Dance Orchestra when it was conducted by Henry Hall?

4 Pierre Fournier is a world-famous musician. What instrument does he play?

5 On which instrument did Bix Beiderbecke make his name?

6 Who was known as 'The Father of English Opera'?

7 What instrument was designed by Bartolommeo Cristofori, in Padua in 1709?

8 Would you be likely to hear a 'tutti' in a concerto? If so, what is it and where would you hear it?

9 Who gave *Othello* a happy ending?

10 Who wrote *The Threepenny Opera*?

11 In the sixteenth century, what was a shawm or schalmey?

12 Which is the lowest string on a violin?

Quiz Seven

General Knowledge

1 What kind of creature is a throstle?

2 What kind of a creature is an erne?

3 *A hooded merganser, to a smew,*
Said: 'Wouldn't it be a bit of luck,
If just the two of us, me and you,
Should meet a friendly goosander duck?'
How many birds are mentioned in that piece of verse?

4 Which is the smallest European sea-bird?

5 What is another name for the lapwing?

6 In Scotland, what kind of creature is a bubbly-jock?

7 What kind of a creature is the adjutant bird?

8 Where does a puffin nest?

9 What kind of creature is a twite?

10 What is the better known name for the land-rail?

11 What kind of creature is a honey-eater?

12 What is the better known name for the solan goose or solent goose?

Quiz Eight
General Knowledge

1 In the sixth century an English kingdom was divided into Bernicia and Deira. What was the kingdom?

2 Which river divided Bernicia and Deira?

3 What is the colour of the ribbon of the French Legion of Honour?

4 What are the colours of the ribbon of the Military Cross?

5 The French and Germans call it St Martin's summer. What do we call it?

6 What sort of a bridge was a clapper bridge?

7 Where would you expect to find a blaze on a horse, if anywhere?

8 Would you use fire to blaze a trail in a forest, or what would you do?

9 What is the name of the Pope's Cathedral Church in Rome?

10 Does a camera have a diaphragm? If so, where is it?

11 What is the unit of currency in Liechtenstein?

12 If a fer-de-lance is not an antique weapon, what is it?

Quiz Eight

Words

1 What does a pteridologist study?

2 Orang-Utans are in danger of extinction. What does the word Orang-Utan mean?

3 How did Napalm get its name?

4 What is a 'joey' to an Australian?

5 Would a canophilist be interested in disciplining young children, paddling canoes, erecting canopies, planting sugar cane – or what?

6 Where would you expect to encounter a xystus? And why?

7 Where would you expect to find cheiromancy (or chiromancy) practised and why?

8 To 'escalate' is a popular – and peculiarly inept – verb with today's Press. Can you say what to 'escalade' means, or meant?

9 Would you say that your hair was scissile?

10 What is a felloe?

11 What is the essential difference between a cathode and an anode?

12 What is the study of fossils called?

Quiz Eight
Geography

1 Can you name the 'twin-city' of Minneapolis, Minnesota?

2 Which is called the 'Windy City' of the USA?

3 What do the Americans mean by 'Big D'?

4 Which is the 'Quaker City' of the USA?

5 Whereabouts are the Shan States?

6 What was the previous name of the country in the East Indies now called Sabah?

7 Which two rivers merge to form the Shatt-al-Arab, in Iraq?

8 What is separated by the Torres Strait?

9 Which country lies to the East of the Gulf of Bothnia?

10 Of which African country is Maseru the capital?

11 Which islands were known as the 'Fortunate Islands'?

12 Which part of the world means, if translated into English – 'Land of Fire'?

Quiz Eight

History

1 In which year was the Royal Flying Corps founded?

2 What was the second-lieutenant in the British Infantry called before 1871?

3 Can you say, to within ten years, when the Military Cross decoration was instituted?

4 Which equivalent fire-arm preceded the rifle in the British army?

5 Can you name one of his four companions who died with Captain Scott on his return journey from the South Pole in 1912?

6 In which year did Yuri Gagarin make his first space flight?

7 Who succeeded Stalin as ruler of the USSR?

8 And what relation is Malenkov to the late Nikita Khrushchev?

9 Who was the first king of Belgium after she became a separate country in 1831?

10 Who was the head of the Cuban Government before Fidel Castro?

11 Who was Foreign Secretary at the outbreak of war on 3 September 1939?

12 Which constituency was represented by Anthony Eden, now Lord Avon, during the whole of his parliamentary career from 1923–57?

Quiz Eight

People

1 Which great dramatist was murdered by Ingram Fraser in 1593?

2 In the official Order of Precedence in England, who ranks highest outside the Royal Family?

3 To what did J. S. Bradbury give his name?

4 Who was the first High Priest of the Jews?

5 Who was Jacob's twin brother?

6 Who was the mother of John the Baptist?

7 Who introduced the Kindergarten system of education, in which very young children are taught by means of objects, games and songs?

8 What was the Lord of Misrule?

9 Who was the Abbot of Unreason?

10 Two Russian engineers, Mikoyan and Gurevich, have given their names to – what?

11 What boon to British and, subsequently, to other road users was invented by Percy Shaw, of Halifax?

12 Who was the original designer of the 'New Look' in 1947?

Quiz Eight

Literature

1 Can you identify the American dramatist who wrote *Mourning Becomes Electra* in 1931, and *The Iceman Cometh* in 1946?

2 Who wrote the successful plays: *Cat on a Hot Tin Roof* and *A Streetcar Named Desire*?

3 He was first the music critic of the *London Star*, and then of *The World*. His first play *Widowers' Houses* was performed in 1892. Who was he?

4 Which Greek playwright complained 2,300 years ago that the young men of his day were: 'Long-haired, half-starved and un-washed'?

5 Thomas Hood wrote in *A Reflection*:
When Eve upon the first of Men
The apple pressed with specious cant,
Oh! what a thousand pities then
That Adam was not ....
Can you supply the missing word?

6 Who wrote the poem: *The Hunting of the Snark*?

7 In Arthurian legend, what was the Siege Perilous?

8 Did anyone ever occupy the Siege Perilous?

9 Over which British kingdom did King Mark rule?

10 What is the connection between the Arthurian *Vivien* and Scott's *Ellen Douglas*?

11 Who wrote the tragedy entitled *The Seven against Thebes*?

12 Who wrote the *Bab Ballads*?

Quiz Eight

Sports and Pastimes

1 What had Jaques Ladoumegue, Jack Lovelock and Glen Cunningham in common?

2 Who was the first racing motorist to raise the car speed record to over 200 miles per hour?

3 Who holds the record for the greatest number of wickets taken during a Test Series?

4 Can you name the captain of the English cricket team in Australia in 1932–3, who introduced 'bodyline' bowling into Test cricket?

5 Who are the Civil Service strollers?

6 What is a 'pair of spectacles' in cricket?

7 Apart from Arsenal in the 1970–71 season, only three football league teams have achieved the FA Cup and League Championship double in the same year since 1888–9, the first season of the Football League. Can you name one of them?

8 According to the rules, what is the official circumference of a soccer ball?

9 Which Association Football club's home ground is at Elland Road?

10 In Association Football, how far is the penalty spot from the nearest part of the goal-line?

11 One of the fastest ball games in the world is played by the Basques with a small ball and a racquet rather like a wine basket. What is the game called?

12 How many teams are there in the First Division of the English Football League?

Quiz Eight
Music

1 Who composed the Sea Symphony?

2 Which composer attempted, with some success, to describe orchestrally the motion of an express train, in *Pacific 231*?

3 In which operetta are the principal characters: Count Danilo Danilovitch and Anna Glavari?

4 Who composed the following operas: *Don Pasquale, La Fille du Régiment, Linda di Chamounix, Lucia di Lammermoor* and *Lucrezia Borgia*?

5 Who are Woglinde, Wellgunde and Flosshilde?

6 Who composed *The Love of Three Oranges*?

7 What is meant by the term 'programme music'?

8 What is the name of the hunch-backed court jester who gave his name to an opera?

9 The march has four beats in a bar, the waltz has three beats in a bar. What has two beats in a bar?

10 Who wrote an opera based on the character of Billy Budd?

11 Who set to music the poem by Alexander Pope which begins: *Where'er you walk, cool gales shall fan the glade*?

12 Which musical instrument, of African origin but improved on in central America, is formed of strips of wood struck by hammers or sticks?

Quiz Eight

General Knowledge

1 Earl in Britain, Comte in France, Conte in Italy. What is the German equivalent?

2 Of which type of wine is Château d'Yquem one of the finest examples?

3 What is the literal meaning of a Freebooter?

4 There was a Census in 1971. When will the next be held?

5 St Cyr in France is equivalent to what in England?

6 D.O.M. is inscribed on bottles of the liqueur Benedictine. What do those initials stand for?

7 What is Spy Wednesday?

8 Mocha gave its name to a fine type of coffee. Where, what or who is or was Mocha?

9 If you encountered a simoon, where would you be likely to be? And what is it?

10 When the *Titanic* sank on her maiden voyage in April 1912 she was the world's largest and most luxurious liner. What was her tonnage? (To the nearest 1,000 tons.)

11 Why does a hubble-bubble bubble?

12 Can you describe a natterjack?

Quiz Nine

General Knowledge

1 What features, still observable on the south-east coast of England, were named after Cape Mortella, in Corsica?

2 What edifice is ascribed to St Hugh of Lincoln?

3 Border Leicester, Kerry Hill, Clun Forest – what are they?

4 What are Morels, Chanterelles and Ceps?

5 When a Japanese says that a friend of his had a happy dispatch, does it mean he had received good news; he had taken off successfully from Tokyo Airport, or what?

6 Who was the author of the epoch-making work *The Discourse on Method*; also Dioptrics; Meteors and Geometry, which are essays on this Method?

7 How does a colporteur earn his living?

8 What is, or was, a minuteman?

9 The sinking of the Cunard liner, *Lusitania,* with the loss of 1198 lives, on 7 May 1915, by a German submarine, was one of the first great marine disasters of the First World War. Can you say, to within 100 miles, where the *Lusitania* went down?

10 Is it true to say that Helsingör is the old name for the capital of Finland? And explain your answer.

11 It is called the 'Wiggentree' in Westmorland, was venerated by the Druids, and was formerly known as the 'Wichen', because it was supposed to ward off witches. What do we call it today?

12 Francis Barraud's fox terrier has been going the rounds for nearly seventy years; which must be a record of some sort. Where would you be likely to see him?

Quiz Nine

Words

1 You may sometimes have told your better half that you are 'worn to a frazzle'. Have you ever worn anything to a frazzle?

2 In the jingle:
If ifs and ans
Were pots and pans
Where would be the tinker?
describing wishful thinking, what is the meaning of the word 'ans'?

3 You have probably said, or read, on occasions, that 'The situation was fraught with danger'. Do you know the original meaning of the word 'fraught'?

4 What is the true meaning of the word sophisticated?

5 What, precisely, is a catalyst?

6 Can you give an example of *lex talionis*?

7 'On the strict Q.T.' means with complete secrecy. What does Q.T. stand for?

8 How can you be in jeopardy if you have an even chance. Can you explain?

9 If you were told that you were a cacographer, would you be pleased or sorry? And why?

10 What is the difference between a naiad and a dryad?

11 What are incunabula?

12 What is an inchoate instrument?

Quiz Nine
Geography

1 Lincoln is the county town of Lincolnshire, England. It is also the capital of one of the States of the USA. Which one?

2 Of which State of the USA is Carson City the capital?

3 What is the capital of the State of Idaho?

4 You are on a river steamer. You look out over the starboard rail and there is Paraguay. You walk across the ship, look out over the port rail and there is the Argentine. On which river are you?

5 What is the name of the Sussex town, a one-time port, which is now about two miles inland?

6 Easter Island lies in the South Pacific Ocean, about 2300 miles west of Chile. To which country does it belong?

7 With which country or countries does Denmark have a common border?

8 Of which African country is Abidjan the capital city?

9 If Shansi, Shensi, Kirin and Kansu are not an oriental firm of solicitors, what are they?

10 Of which country is Mogadishu the capital?

11 For administrative purposes, Italy is divided in 19 regions, e.g. Sicily, Piedmont, Sardinia, etc. Do you know, or can you guess, which is the largest Italian region, in area?

12 On which river is Leningrad situated?

Quiz Nine

History

1 Blenheim, Ramillies and Malplaquet. Which one is missing?

2 Who was nicknamed 'Old Rowley'? And why?

3 Who was the first English monarch to be styled His (or Her) Majesty?

4 Which was the last English monarch to die a violent and unnatural death?

5 Edward Hyde, who lived from 1609–74, had two granddaughters who both became Queens of Great Britain. Can you name them both?

6 We have just mentioned Edward Hyde, who later became the First Earl of Clarendon. What is his connection with Hyde Park?

7 Which famous American was born in Hyde Park?

8 Can you say to within five years when the Whigs changed their name to Liberals?

9 When did the Tories change their name to the Conservatives?

10 Which English king was nicknamed 'Beauclerc' and why?

11 Who was the first Duke of Cornwall?

12 Whereabouts, according to tradition, was King Arthur born?

Quiz Nine

People

1 Which famous MP represented the Ebbw Vale constituency from 1929–60?

2 What method of communication was invented by Dr L. L. Zamenhof of Warsaw in 1887?

3 What charitable movement was founded by Paul Harris, in Chicago, in 1905?

4 Who started in Newtown, then moved to Wyvern, and now operates in Thamesford?

5 Which well-known sculptor was responsible for the lions at the foot of Nelson's Column in Trafalgar Square?

6 Who is the Metropolitan of the Northern Province of England?

7 Who is the Primate of England?

8 Who received the Oscar for the best actress of the year in 1971?

9 Who was the King of Lydia whose name became synonymous with riches?

10 Who was the first woman on earth, according to Greek mythology?

11 Who was the wife of Orpheus?

12 Who, in German legend, is the Erlking?

Quiz Nine

Literature

1 What is the connection between Nicholas Nickleby and Barnard Castle?

2 What is the title of the series of works by William Cobbett, published in 1830, describing his personal investigations into the agricultural conditions of his day?

3 Who was the female member of Fagin's gang of thieves in Charles Dickens's *Oliver Twist*?

4 Who wrote the story of Trilby (and Svengali)?

5 Who was the Poet Laureate from 1930–1968, when he was succeeded by Cecil Day Lewis?

6 Which twentieth-century poet, an OM and a Nobel Prize winner, wrote *Prufrock*, *The Waste Land* and *Four Quartets*?

7 Who was the first official Poet Laureate of this country?

8 Can you say how Dickens acquired the pseudonym, 'Boz'?

9 According to Kipling's *Smuggler's Song*:
Five and twenty ponies
Trotting through the dark –
Brandy for the Parson
Baccy for the Clerk;
Can you mention one of the other two commodities they were carrying?

10 In Dickens's *Bleak House*, what was Mrs Jellyby's besetting sin?

11 As whom is the novelist, Lady Frederick Browning, better known?

12 Who was Maggie Tulliver?

Quiz Nine
Sports and Pastimes

1 At Iffley Road Track, Oxford, Roger Bannister was the first to run the mile in under four minutes. Which year was it?

2 Where will the next Commonwealth Games be held?

3 For which feat did the late Lilian Board receive the silver medal at the Olympic Games in Mexico in 1968?

4 What was Jess Willard's claim to fame?

5 How many players are there in a lacrosse team?

6 In cricket how are bonus bowling points calculated?

7 Which county won the John Player League and the Gillette Cup in 1970?

8 To a racing man, each year, which is 'the last of the Classics'?

9 Over what distance is the Grand National run?

10 What did Nijinsky do in 1970 which was last done by Bahram in 1935?

11 What have Larkspur, Psidium and Relko in common?

12 In squash rackets, if one player impedes his opponent unduly, a 'let' is called. Why is it called a 'let'?

Quiz Nine

Music

1 Louis Armstrong, the world-renowned jazz trumpeter, was nicknamed 'Satch-Mo'. What does Satch-Mo mean?

2 In the first act of a popular Italian opera, reference is made to the 'Star-spangled banner'. Which opera is this?

3 What connection had Cesare Sterbini with Rossini?

4 What have Vaughan Williams' Second Symphony and Haydn's 104th in common?

5 Musically speaking, who, what or where is Sparafucile?

6 *The Witch's Curse*, *The Peer and the Peri*, and *The Merryman and his Maid* are operas by Gilbert and Sullivan. What are the more popular titles?

7 What is the number of Dvořák's *New World Symphony*?

8 Which present-day composer wrote the oratorio, *A Child of our Time*?

9 The ukulele is a kind of small guitar. In which country did it originate?

10 What is the better-known name for Beethoven's Piano Sonata in F Minor, Opus 57?

11 Who founded the London Philharmonic Orchestra in 1932?

12 Which old Celtic musical instrument has the same name as an English dance?

Quiz Nine

General Knowledge

1 Why did the Germans call their doodle-bugs V-1's and V-2's?

2 The Palladium and the Coliseum in London are both centres of entertainment. Can you say why 'Palladium' is a misnomer?

3 Roughly how many inhabitants has the Commonwealth?

4 The Prince of Wales is first in the Order of Succession to the Throne. Who is second?

5 Of which English family is Chatsworth, Derbyshire, the country seat?

6 What was a Hecatomb – and we want an exact answer?

7 If I were to tell you that you could speak the language of the American Ojibway Indians, you would probably deny it. But you can. You know, for instance, I am sure, the Ojibway words for Great River. What are they?

8 If, in the Middle Ages, a man would have approached you with a morning star, would you have accepted it gratefully? Would you have taken him to the nearest monastery for a prayer of thanksgiving? Would you have plucked and cooked it, or would you have run away? And explain your answer.

9 Apart from pies and sausages, what is the best-known product of Melton Mowbray?

10 As what are the Twelve Peers of Charlemagne's Court better known?

11 In which English seaport is the beautiful parish church of St Mary Redcliffe, described by Queen Elizabeth I as 'the fairest and most goodliest parish church in all my realm'?

12 The size, weight and contents of a sandwich served to you free on board an airliner is regulated by IATA. Who or what is IATA?

Answers

Quiz One

General Knowledge

1 They'd never heard of it! The potato was not introduced into Europe from America until the mid-sixteenth century, some say by Sir Walter Raleigh. The Latin name given to the potato is *Solanum tuberosum*, which means literally, 'The bulb of the nightshade' and sounds most unappetising!

2 Because Raleigh introduced it into Ireland first, whence it came to England, where it later became a 'Murphy' after the common Irish surname. (Many authorities claim that it was introduced into Spain before Raleigh brought it to Ireland.)

3 The Khedive was the title accorded to Ismail Pasha, as Viceroy of Egypt, by the Turkish Government in 1867. It was abolished in 1914. (The word is Turkish, from Persian, and means 'a Prince'.)

4 The name has nothing to do with any Charles. It is a corruption of 'Churl's wain' – a peasant cart.

5 They were the first four manned American spacecraft.

6 It was a reckless mania for the purchase of tulip bulbs, which reached its height in Holland about 1634–1637. A bulb of the species 'Viceroy' sold for £250; 'Semper Augustus' for £500, and this manic speculation spread all over Europe.

7 A kind of two-ply or ingrain carpet, originally manufactured in Kidderminster.

8 Diploma of Public Health. Usually after the name of a doctor.

9 The Sea of Marmara, between the Bosphorus and the Dardanelles.

10 Godalming, Surrey.

11 To airline pilots (and their passengers). They are all English and Welsh airports (Lulsgate serves Bristol, Rhoose – Cardiff, Yeadon serves Leeds and Bradford, and Woolsington serves Newcastle).

12 Hebrew language and learning.

Words

1 He is a Spanish nobleman.

2 It is a land measure of considerable antiquity, stretching back well
before the Domesday survey, and of indeterminate area. Most of
such ancient measures were fractions of a hide of land, and as the
area of the hide differed in different parts of the country, it is
impossible to be precise, but some authorities claim it to be one
quarter of a hide of 120 acres, or 30 acres.

3 The measurement of the intensity of light.

4 It was a nightmare, even earlier, a demon who was supposed to
obsess people in their sleep.

5 A sacred carving. The hieroglyphic script was first used by the
Egyptian priests about 3,500 BC.

6 A member of the barmecides, a wealthy Persian family which
furnished courtiers to Harum Al-Rashid, an early Caliph of Baghdad.
(In the Arabian Nights, the story is told of a barmecide who invited
a hungry beggar to a feast at which he made a pretence of serving
and eating imaginary food. In this the beggar good-naturedly joined
in, and was rewarded by a real feast. Hence Barmecide Feast – an
illusion of plenty.)

7 It was a password – coined by Hephthah to enable him to catch the
fleeing Ephraimites, who couldn't pronounce 'sh'. When they reached
a ford on the Jordan, they gave the password as 'Sibboleth', which
gave them away. It was used as a test to distinguish the Gilealites
(Hephthah's own men) from the Ephraimites.

8 The shambles were the stalls on which butchers exposed their meat
for sale, hence a flesh market, a slaughter house, a scene of carnage.

9 It is a false assertion by a person of being married to another (which,
in certain circumstances, is actionable).

10 A ferrule was, and is, a metal band or cap to protect or strengthen
the end of a stick or tube, i.e., the wooden end of a walking-stick or
umbrella. A ferule was a flat ruler with a widened end for chastising
boys.

11 The muscle in it. The word muscle derives from the Latin *musculus* – a little mouse, because certain muscle movements resemble the darting movements of mice.

12 It is an egocentric philosophy, based on the theory that self-existence is the only certainty.

Geography

1 In northern Argyllshire, two miles east of Ballachulish and south of Loch Leven.

2 These are the Scottish Don and Dee. The county is Aberdeenshire.

3 No. Holland is one of the administrative divisions of Lincolnshire. Spalding is in the south-west of it. Lindsey and Kesteven are the other two administrative divisions of Lincolnshire.

4 In the Pentland Firth between Orkney and the Scottish mainland. The Merry Men of May is an expanse of broken water which boils like a cauldron on the southern side of the Stroma Channel – off the coast of Caithness.

5 Mainland, Yell, Unst, and Fetlar.

6 Northamptonshire. It is twelve miles north-north-west of Northampton.

7 No. It is inaccurate, not because *this* Dorchester is in Dorset, but because it is on the River Thame, just before this tributary flows into the Thames. Dorchester is now a village eight miles south-east of Oxford with a population of about 800.

8 Dorset – but covering also the whole of the old Kingdom of Wessex: Berkshire, Wiltshire, Somerset, Hampshire and Devon.

9 Twelve. Anglesey (the Island county), Brecon (or Brecknock), Caernarvon, Cardigan, Carmarthen, Denbigh, Flint, Glamorgan, Merioneth, Montgomery, Pembroke and Radnor.

10 Suffolk. At Lowestoft Ness, one mile east of Lowestoft. 1°48′ E.

11 Tower Bridge. There are tunnels at Rotherhithe, Blackwall and Dartford, but no more bridges below Tower Bridge.

12 In Montgomeryshire. The River Severn (220 miles) rises about two miles north-east of Plynlimon.

History

1 Sir Alec Douglas-Home. They are the Prime Ministers since the beginning of the Second World War.

2 1924.

3 Ministry of Labour.

4 General Kurt von Schleicher (1882–1934). Von Papen (1879–1969) was Chancellor from 31 May 1932 until his resignation on 17 November 1932. Von Schleicher was Chancellor from 2 December 1932 until 28 January 1933.

5 Dr Kurt Kiesinger.

6 Pandit Jawaharlal Nehru, in 1947–64.

7 Lidice.

8 The British evacuation from Dunkirk. (The allied invasion of Northern Europe was 'Operation Overlord'.)

9 8 May 1945.

10 15 June 1945. Over nine and a half years and the longest Parliament of modern times. During the two World Wars the five years' period was prolonged, in the First World War Parliament met for seven years nine months, and in the Second World War, just over nine years six months. The Prime Ministers during this period were Baldwin, Chamberlain and Winston Churchill.

11 Joseph Chamberlain. (He was a Cabinet Minister in two Governments, as President of the Board of Trade under Gladstone, and Secretary for the Colonies under Lord Salisbury. But he was a bit too radical for his time and never reached the top.)

12 The then Air Chief Marshal Arthur William Tedder.

People

1 Pele, the incomparable Brazilian footballer.

2 Dame Clara Butt, the famous contralto of the early twentieth century. She was made a D.B.E. in 1920.

3 Albert, Duke of Clarence and Avondale, and Earl of Athlone. He was born in 1864 and died in 1892 after a short illness, whilst his father was still Prince of Wales.

4 C. B. Fry (Charles Burgess Fry, 1872–1956). After his seventieth birthday, it is reported, he told a friend that, looking for new worlds to conquer, he was proposing to interest himself in the turf and to attach himself to a stable. His friend, succinctly summing up his life-long versatility, replied: 'In what capacity, Charles, trainer, jockey or horse?'

5 Lord (Baron) Beaverbrook.

6 Trotsky (1879–1940). His full name was Lev Davidovich Bronstein.

7 Lenin (1870–1924), whose real name was Vladimir Ilyich Ulyanov.

8 Count Ciano.

9 He is a French playwright and film-writer.

10 Auguste and Jean Piccard are Swiss physicists who became famous for their balloon ascents into the stratosphere and deep descents into the ocean in a bathyscaphe, in the 1930s and after the war.

11 Gladys Aylward.

12 She was the American founder of the Christian Science movement.

Literature

1 'Dotheboys Hall', in Dickens's *Nicholas Nickleby*, of which supposed educational establishment Squeers was the brutal and ignorant master.

2 (George) Emlyn Williams.

3 With his cross-bow.
God save thee, ancient Mariner!
from the fiends that plague thee thus! –
Why look'st thou so? – with my cross-bow
I shot the albatross.

4 Ella Wheeler Wilcox, the American poet and journalist, who was described by *The Times* in 1919 as 'The most popular poet of either sex and of any age, read by thousands who never open Shakespeare!'

5 Sir Richard Grenville, according to Tennyson, in *The Revenge*.

6 'Mrs Helen Graham' or more correctly, 'Mrs Helen Huntingdon'.

7 In Luggnagg.

8 *The Good Companions*, by J. B. Priestley.

9 They are two classic collections of early Icelandic literature, which constitute today our chief source of information about Scandinavian mythology. (The Older Edda is a collection of Norwegian poems of the ninth to twelfth centuries. The Younger Edda is a chiefly prose work largely concerned with ancient Scandinavian religion, written in the thirteenth century.

10 *The Chiltern Hundreds* is one of the successful plays written by William Douglas-Home, younger brother of Sir Alec Douglas-Home.

11 Largely by the martial novel *Beau Geste* (1924), dealing with the French Foreign Legion, which was subsequently made into a successful film. He also wrote *Beau Sabreur* and other novels.

12 To write the most amusing, original and incomparable history of England ever attempted. They called it *1066 and All That*. (They also wrote three other nonsense novels, *And Now All This*, *Horse Nonsense* and *Garden Rubbish*, all in the early 1930s.)

Sports and Pastimes

1 There is none! In cricket a googly is an off-break bowled with a leg-break action, the etymology of the word googly being unknown. The Australians, more logically, called it a bosey after B. J. T. Bosanquet, the inventor.

2 Eddie Barlow, of South Africa.

3 'Sundries'.

4 One batting point is awarded for every twenty-five runs scored in excess of 150, in the first eighty-five overs (first innings).

5 Take a stroke when you felt like it. A bisque at golf is the right to deduct a stroke from your score at any hole you choose. (At tennis you can claim a free point at any time; and at croquet it entitles you to play an extra turn.)

6 It is the trophy for which England and Scotland play Rugby Union Football annually, at Twickenham or Murrayfield. It was presented by the Calcutta Club, India, in 1879.

7 She achieved the elusive 'grand slam' of holding the four world's major women's lawn tennis singles titles (Wimbledon, USA, Australian and French) at the same time.

8 Maureen (Little Mo) Connolly, of the USA.

9 Eleven.

10 A skater – they are jumps used in figure skating.

11 Nine (a pitcher, a catcher, four fielders, three outfielders. Possibly derived from cricket and rounders).

12 In the fifteenth round.

Music

1 Bruno Walter, the famous German-born conductor, who took French nationality in 1938 and settled in the USA in 1939. He died in California in 1962.

2 The late Sir Malcolm Sargent, the well-loved conductor, pianist and organist.

3 He was a famous American band leader of the late 1920s and early 30s.

4 Edward Kennedy (Duke) Ellington. One of the great band leaders of all time.

5 Irving Berlin. A man with a string of successes commencing with *Alexander's Ragtime Band* in 1911, and including the ubiquitous and inescapable *White Christmas* which has sold more gramophone records than any other.

6 Elizabeth Schwarzkopf, the incomparable German soprano, in both opera and lieder.

7 Damon Runyon, 1884–1946.

8 Prokofiev. The libretto was by Mira Mendelson.

9 Patience, after whom the opera is named. Its alternative title is *Bunthorne's Bride*.

10 Delibes.

11 In singing. It is the practice – for long frowned upon by the purists – of inserting the aspirate amongst vowel sounds, particularly in runs on one vowel. This frequently occurs in oratorio singing. An example might be: 'and the trumpe(h)et sha(h)all sound, and the dead sha(h)all be(h)e raised . . .'

12 Verdi's.

General Knowledge

1 Most probably to an antique dealer. A spoon-back was a Queen Anne chair with a back like the curve of a spoon.

2 All motor vehicles prohibited.

3 Queen Elizabeth the Queen mother. Apart from HM the Queen, who is sovereign of the order, the Queen mother is the only female holder of the order.

4 Midnight to 4 am, which is also called midwatch – and mid-to-four watch.

5 It is the third annual term of the English law sittings. (From the first Tuesday after Trinity Sunday until 31 July.)

6 Chief Officer. (In Scotland the same position carries the title of Fire Master.)

7 Rustic Chivalry.

8 Hungary. It is the Hungarian currency.

9 Those of Wiltshire: Indicating simplicity, because, according to outsiders, 'some Wiltshire rustics, seeing the reflection of the moon in a pond, attempted to rake it out'. Any true Wiltshireman will tell you they were raking the pond for smuggled brandy kegs, and fooled the excisemen by pretending to this folly.

10 The New Testament tares are thought by many authorities to have been the bearded darnel. Not until the tares ripen and grow yellow can they be distinguished from the wheat amongst which they grow, hence the practical advice of the householder in the parable to allow both to grow together until the harvest.

11 His food. Tucker, for food, especially that carried on a long journey, is the Australian equivalent of the English schoolboy slang word *tuck* for a private store of food.

12 It was the (detachable) front part of a gun-carriage consisting of two wheels, axle, ammunition-box, and the shaft to which the horses were attached.

Quiz Two

General Knowledge

1 It is the rope used to tie up a small boat.

2 They were the armorial bearings of the Medici family, richest of the Lombardy merchant princes. (Banking, although the Lombardy Street moguls hate to admit it, is only a glorified form of pawnbroking, and the original Italian merchants in the London Street named after them frequently displayed this sign. After the Banks became 'respectable', the pawnbrokers took it over.)

3 Sesame is an Asian herb with oily edible seeds; 'open sesame!' was the password which opened the door of the robbers' cave in *The Arabian Nights*; and *Sesame and Lilies* were two very popular lectures published by Ruskin in 1865.

4 Lisle (thread). Originally made at Lille, capital of the Nord department. (It is interesting to note that our spelling, *Lisle*, is more historically accurate than the French, *Lille*. Its original name was *l'Isle*, the island, from its remote position amongst the marshes which once obtained in this part of France.)

5 Exactly 38 mph. 1 nautical mile equals 1·1515 statute land miles, so 1 knot or nautical mph equals 1·1515 land mph. The knot is a measure of speed, not distance. One never says 'so many knots per hour'.

6 Twenty-four.

7 It literally means Ministry for Internal Affairs (Ministerstvo Vnutrennykh Del). In fact, it means the Russian political police.

8 It is a ram of the Cheviot breed of sheep, originating on the English/ Scottish border. The female is called a dam. Tup and dam are synonymous with ram and ewe.

9 Thirty-five years.

10 The House of Representatives votes on the five candidates with the highest number of electoral votes (each State Delegation casting one vote).

11 Pomanders.

12 The egg-case of the ray, skate, shark, or dog-fish.

Words

1 It is a female porter. (If and when she is introduced by British Rail).

2 Probably because an Egyptian Pharaoh was depicted on one of the cards.

3 Caves, and their contents.

4 He was a stone-breaker, for road-making, formerly to be seen seated beside the highway with a pile of flints, a large hammer, and wearing goggles to protect his eyes. (Also a knapping-hammer – used for breaking stones for road-making.)

5 A strath is a broad valley between the mountains, with a river running through it. A glen is a narrow valley in the mountains with or without a river.

6 Extrinsic means outside, not belonging. Intrinsic means belonging naturally – inherent.

7 Nothing – they both mean the process of collecting into a mass – a confused mass of various objects.

8 An isobar is a line on a weather chart, linking places with the same atmospheric pressure. An isotherm links places with the same temperature.

9 To shackle, or to confine. Hence untrammelled – unhampered.

10 Probably to the choir stall of a church or cathedral. To cantillate means to chant, or intone in free rhythm, in plainsong.

11 Simony.

12 A tréma. (Diaeresis: the division of one syllable into two. The two dots ¨ marking such a division.)

Geography

1 It is a district of Romania bounded by the Carpathian Mountains and the Transylvanian Alps.

2 They are all cities of Iran.

3 In Sierra Leone – it is the capital. Also a rural town in south-east Massachusetts, USA.

4 Greenland and Iceland.

5 Dinant is a Belgian tourist centre on the River Meuse, forty-five miles south-east of Brussels. (Thirty miles south-west of Liège). Dinan is an ancient town and holiday resort in Brittany, fourteen miles south of St Malo.

6 Senegal.

7 Guyana.

8 New Brunswick.

9 Pyongyang.

10 The Ligurian sea (between Corsica and North Italy), the Tyrrhenian sea (bordered by Sardinia, S. Italy and Sicily), and the Ionian sea (between the foot of Italy and Greece, south of the Strait of Otranto).

11 Hawaii, Oahu (containing Honolulu, and Pearl Harbour), Maui, Kauai, Molokai, Lanai, Niihau and Kahoolawa.

12 The Central American Republic of Honduras. (Not British Honduras, the capital of which is Belize.)

History

1 Williams. Cromwell's great-grandfather married Katharine, eldest sister of Thomas Cromwell, Earl of Essex (1485–1540), and took his wife's name. In his marriage settlement, Cromwell is called 'Oliver Cromwell, alias Williams'.

2 Near the site of the battle at Senlac, called Battle Abbey, part of which is now a girls' school. The village of Battle grew up around it.

3 The other three were: Haselrig, Strode and Holles.

4 Richard, Duke of York, one of the princes murdered in the Tower.

5 Canterbury.

6 King Edward the Martyr (son of Edgar), when only in his teens, probably by his step-mother, to secure the throne for his half-brother, Ethelred the Unready.

7 King Harold Hardrada of Norway. The English King Harold, beat him at Stamford Bridge – and marched south again to take on William the Conqueror.

8 Katherine of Aragon, first wife of Henry VIII.

9 Edmund Tudor, first Earl of Richmond, and son of Owen Tudor.

10 Sir John Hawkins. (He was buried at sea off Puerto Rico.)

11 King James I (James VI of Scotland) (1603–1625). Shakespeare died in 1616.

12 Canute.

People

1 The American General George S. Patton.

2 Psalmanazar was the assumed name of a Frenchman who came to London in 1703, claiming to be a native of Formosa. He published an account of the island with a grammar of the language. It was a complete fabrication, but the literary and critical world of London was taken in. Later, he confessed his fraud, and applied himself to the study of Hebrew and other genuine work, and ended his days in 1763 as a man of some repute, and the friend of Dr Johnson.

3 Dan Leno.

4 John Buchan (1875–1940), the Scottish author, historian and statesman. Created Lord Tweedsmuir when he was appointed Governor General of Canada.

5 Thomas De Quincey (1785–1859), in his book *Confessions of an English Opium-eater*. At one time he was taking 8,000 drops of laudanum a day. By a great effort, involving considerable physical affliction, he had practically conquered his addiction before he died.

6 King George VI. The Dukedom of York is frequently conferred upon the second or later son of an English king: e.g. King George V, second son of Edward VII, and King George VI, second son of George V.

7 The Sioux. He commanded the Indians who cut General Custer's army to pieces at Little Big Horn in 1876.

8 Haydn (The Emperor was, of course, the Austrian Emperor).

9 Alicia Markova, the famous ballet dancer. (She was the first English 'Prima Ballerina Assoluta' in history). Now Dame Alicia Markova.

10 Edgar Allan Poe (1809–49) was a US citizen, born in Boston.

11 Tennessee Williams, the famous playwright.

12 Prince Philip – The Duke of Edinburgh; the Duke of Windsor; and the Duke of Gloucester.

Literature

1 In a way, the Jerusalem Chamber was the Chapter House of Westminster Abbey and Henry IV died there in March 1413. The remainder of the quotation is:
Which, verily, I supposed the Holy Land:
But bear me to that chamber; there I'll lie;
In that Jerusalem shall Harry die!

2 The 'Two gentlemen of Verona' in Shakespeare's play.

3 Moth.

4 Malvolio.

5 Marcellus, to Horatio, on the guard-platform of Elsinore Castle, after Hamlet and the ghost had left.

6 King Henry IV, part II.

7 Ophelia's.

8 Tongues.
Finds tongues in trees, books in the running brooks,
Sermons in stones, and good in everything.

9 Sir Oliver Martext.

10 The Ghost of Hamlet's father.

11 A dew.

> *O, that this too, too solid flesh would melt,*
> *Thaw and resolve itself into a dew.*

12 Othello. Brabantio was the father of Desdemona.

Sports and Pastimes

1 Cardiff. They beat Arsenal at Wembley in 1927.

2 Red and white. They wear red shirts with white collars and cuffs, white shorts, red socks with white tops.

3 Wakefield Trinity is a Rugby League Football Club.

4 They are American Baseball Clubs: California Angels, Cleveland Indians, Chicago Whitesox and Detroit Tigers.

5 Australia. The sport was introduced to Britain in February 1928.

6 They are a series of cannons made at billiards, played so that the balls move as little as possible.

7 Racing motorists. It is a race which takes place in Indianapolis every year.

8 A pigeon fancier. Rollers, tipplers and tumblers are types of racing pigeons.

9 Marbles. A tolley is a marble, the ring is a pitch, and a fudge is a flick of the wrist, which constitutes a foul.

10 Twenty-two. 15 reds: 1 yellow: 1 green: 1 brown: 1 blue: 1 pink: 1 black and 1 white.

11 William Gilbert.

12 Twenty-eight.

Music

1 The harpsichord. *Cembalo* was Italian for the dulcimer and the Italians called the harpsichord *clavicembalo* or keyed dulcimer, which soon became re-abbreviated to *cembalo*.

2 The piccolo, or octave flute.

3 The fifth of the scale.

4 Parsifal.

5 It is the sign: sharp, flat, natural, etc., indicating (momentary) departure from the key signature, which holds good throughout the bar, unless contradicted.

6 On the harp. A homophone is two strings tuned to produce the same note.

7 Mutes raised, or taken off (the violin, etc.).

8 The opera is *L'Elisir d'Amore* (The Love Potion) by Donizetti (1797–1848).

9 He wrote the words of *Land of Hope and Glory* set to the music of part of Elgar's *Pomp and Circumstance March* No. 1.

10 It is not an instrument at all. It is a type of music for the bagpipes, usually martial, and in memory of some historical event.

11 A musical instrument – a kind of lute – with two necks and two sets of tuning pegs.

12 A cradle-song, or lullaby.

General Knowledge

1 The ptarmigan and the willow grouse. Except for a black tail which is largely hidden by white tail-coverts when at rest. The male ptarmigan also has a small black face patch between bill and eye, but you have to get pretty close to notice it. The willow grouse is seldom seen in this country.

2 The moa, related to the ostrich. It was sometimes twelve feet tall.

3 There are no ostriches in Argentina; except in zoos. Ostriches are native to Africa and Arabia.

4 False. Horses do not suffer from foot-and-mouth disease.

5 It is the largest living rodent. It is about four feet long, weighs up to a hundred pounds, has a large stumpy head and a very short tail.

6 The king cobra (*Ophiophagus Hannah*).

7 The burbot, or eel-pout. It is shaped like an eel, but shorter, with two small barbs on the nose and another on the chin.

8 Cook and eat them. They are edible shell-fish. In the UK they are found only in the Channel Islands and are also known as sea-ears because they are said to resemble a human ear.

9 It is the fluid from the 'ink-bag' of a few species of cuttle-fish.

10 The common sturgeon (*Acipenser sturio*). A female of 460 lb. was taken in the River Esk, Yorkshire, in 1810, and there is an unsubstantiated claim for one of 'over 500 lb.' from the River Severn in 1937.

11 It is a provincial and old poetic name for the lark.

12 The emu (the largest is the ostrich).

Quiz Three Answers

General Knowledge

1 Oedipus.

2 It was posed in varying versions down the ages, one of which is:
What goes on four feet, or two feet, and three,
But the more feet it goes on the weaker it be?
And the answer, given by Oedipus, was Man, who crawls on all-fours as an infant, stands erect on two feet in manhood and resorts to a crutch or staff in old age.

3 The first of March.

4 It is the ancient palace of the Spanish sovereigns, containing also a monastery, church and mausoleum. It is about twenty-seven miles north-west of Madrid.

5 They are each old Scots liquid measures. (A mutchkin equalled three-quarters of an imperial pint. A chopin was 1 imperial quart.)

6 Because a trencher was the wooden platter on which food was cut at meals, thence the plate from which it was eaten. So, he who was good with the trencher ate the lot.

7 2 lb. $3\frac{1}{2}$ oz. approximately.

8 It's a piece of rock-drilling equipment in which the drill is raised by a cable and allowed to drop.

9 A churn drill.

10 Either in a zoo or on a visit overseas. A tylopod is an animal with padded, rather than hoofed digits, such as a camel.

11 Orchids.

12 Storm (10: Whole Gale; 12: Hurricane).

Words

1 It is a kind of salamander, found in lakes near Mexico City.

2 An instrument used to locate the position of optical axes, especially one used to adjust a pair of spectacles properly with respect to the axes of the eyes.

3 It depends entirely upon what sort of a person you are. Mansuetude means gentleness.

4 'Muster' was an army term for the assembly of troops for inspection. If a soldier 'passed muster', he passed the inspection uncensored.

5 A cutter of stones, or inscriptions on stones.

6 Fine inlay work in gold and silver on iron or steel (first practised in Damascus – hence the name).

7 Any large one, especially a cedar. Umbriferous means casting a shadow; affording shade.

8 It is hooked, like an eagle's beak.

9 Seasonable. In tide, in season, in time. We retain this meaning of tide in 'eventide', 'Eastertide', etc. The etymology seems to be that things done punctually and in their proper season are orderly, and what is orderly is neat and well arranged.

10 It is the end of a weaver's thread; or the fringe of threads remaining on a loom when the web has been cut off.

11 It is a handbook, pocket companion, etc., constantly carried with one (from Latin *vade* – go, *mecum* – with me). The expression was more popular fifty years ago than today.

12 It is the use of an epithet for a proper name, e.g. 'The Iron Duke' for the Duke of Wellington, or conversely, the use of a proper name to express a general idea: 'A Napoleon of finance'; 'A Solomon come to judgement'.

Geography

1 The River Volga, 2,400 miles.

2 The Andes (Cordillera de los Andes): 4,500 miles. Other long ranges are the Rocky Mountains: 3,750 miles, and the Himalaya-Karakoram-Hindu Kush range: 2,400 miles.

3 Duisburg, in West Germany, at the junction of the Rhine and the Ruhr.

4 A way to the East from Europe through the Arctic round the north extremity of Asia (USSR).

5 The Moluccas, now part of Indonesia. In the Malay Archipelago, they have been famous for hundreds of years for the production of spices of all kinds.

6 Senegal.

7 They are all tributaries of the Mississippi river.

8 Astrakhan.

9 It is in north-east Italy, running some forty miles from the Appenines across the coastal plain to the Adriatic some seven miles north-west of Rimini. It marked the border between the Roman Republic and Cisalpine Gaul, and when Julius Caesar crossed it, he technically invaded the republic.

10 Algeria. Sidi-Bel-Abbes was once famous as the headquarters of the French Foreign Legion.

11 Ibiza. (Minorca is north-east of Majorca.) (Also Formentera – just off and south of Ibiza.)

12 Lake Ladoga, in the USSR, just north-east of Leningrad. Area about 7,000 square miles.

History

1 1603. When James VI of Scotland acceded to the throne of England as James I.

2 It could only be King John (of England), couldn't it? He achieved this nadir of his career – and that took some doing! – on 15 May 1213.

3 At the Parsonage House, Burnham Thorpe, in the county of Norfolk, where his father was rector.

4 Nelson never lost his right leg. He lost his right arm at Santa Cruz de Teneriffe in July 1797.

5 They were Archbishop Sancroft, eight bishops and four hundred clergymen who, after the revolution of 1688, refused to take the oath of allegiance to William and Mary. They existed as a rival church, consecrating their own bishops, the last of whom died in 1805.

6 Edward I (*c*. 1284).

7 King Richard II.

8 King Louis XIV, also nicknamed 'Le Grand Monarque'.

9 King Richard II of England.

10 King Richard II. He was called Richard of Bordeaux because he was born there in 1367.

11 Sir Henry Percy, son of Henry Percy, first Earl of Northumberland.

12 A revolutionary labour organisation of the early twentieth century – especially in the USA – commonly called the IWW (Industrial Workers of the World) or the 'Wobblies'.

People

1 A famous German writer, composer, storyteller, dramatist, and lawyer (1776–1822). He wrote the fatalistic demonic novel *The Devil's Elixir* (1815–16).

2 Ibsen.

3 Vincent.

4 Dr Alfred Adler (1870–1937). He worked with Freud from 1900–1910, but did not accept some of the more dogmatic Freudian theories and they parted company. In one of his books – *Organic Inferiority and Psychic Compensation* – he advanced the 'inferiority complex' theory.

5 Charles Farrar Browne, the great American humorist, who lived from 1834–1867.

6 George Orwell (*1984, Animal Farm*, etc.).

7 Lord Byron, in 1815. He left her in 1816!

8 John Milton.

9 1950 (15 August).

10 In Oxfordshire, at Blenheim Palace.

11 The Marx Brothers, famous American film comedians. Julius – Groucho, Arthur – Harpo, Leonard – Chico, and Herbert – Zeppo. (Another brother, Milton – Gummo, occasionally appeared.)

12 The statement is correct – but the winner was Ernie Piggott, Lester Piggott's grandfather, who won in 1912. Lester Piggott is a flat-race jockey.

Literature

1 *La Dame Aux Camélias*.

2 Ilium.

3 Mrs Hudson.

4 Jane Austen (1775–1817).

5 *The Herries Chronicle* (published 1930–33).

6 Charles Dickens.

7 The county of 'Glorious Devon'. Set to music by Edward German.

8 Sir Arthur Pinero, in 1893.

9 Ebenezer.

10 Edmund Spenser (1522–99) named Queen Elizabeth so.

11 He wrote the plays *Madame Butterfly* and *The Girl of the Golden West*, which served Puccini as libretti for two of his operas.

12 Terence Rattigan.

Sports and Pastimes

1 Seven.

2 Burnley.

3 Millwall.

4 Everton.

5 They are all defunct Football League clubs (although still playing in minor leagues).

6 There is no maximum weight. A heavyweight can be any weight over 175 lb., or 12 st. 7 lb.

7 Dormy is the expression used when one player cannot lose – e.g. if he is leading his opponent by two and there are only two holes left to play.

8 He won the men's singles championship at Wimbledon. Rockhampton, in Queensland, was the home of Rod Laver.

9 The 50-kilometre walk, which is 31·07 miles (the marathon is only 26 miles 385 yards).

10 Hampden Park, Glasgow, with 149,547.

11 Marbles.

12 Arkle. Archive and Bright Cherry were sire and dam of the famous racehorse.

Music

1 Sinding (1856–1941) was Norwegian.

2 *Greensleeves*.

3 Haydn (Op. 64, No. 5).

4 Verdi (first produced in Venice 1857).

5 King George I. Frequently said to have been first performed on a boat following the Royal Barge on a 'Royal Progress' down the Thames in 1715, but this is dubious.

6 Sir Arthur Sullivan. They are two of the lesser known of the Gilbert and Sullivan comic operas.

7 *The Beggar's Opera* by John Gay.

8 The operas are *A Life for the Czar*, *Russlan and Ludmilla*.

9 Edvard Grieg, in 1875. It was later arranged as two orchestral suites.

10 Igor Stravinsky.

11 They are shaken with the hand. Grelots are small sleigh-bells.

12 The triangle.

General Knowledge

1 'Birmingham Small Arms' Company. Founded in 1861 it was the largest private arms company in the Empire, supplying most of the arms for the Boer War and the First World War. Subsequently it turned principally to cycles and motor-cycles.

2 They were once the same thing. The origin of the word is thought to be from the Hindi, *gend-khana*, a ball or racket house. Nowadays, of course, it is a display or competition of horseriding and jumping.

3 Birmingham; some seventy miles to the east.

4 When it was the boss, or knob, in the centre of his shield, which is what an umbo is, or was.

5 It is the amount set aside in the Civil List (the annual income voted by Parliament to the Crown) for the monarch's personal expenses. It is not the Civil List itself.

6 It was the payment of wages in goods or otherwise than in cash, and was much abused. Various Truck Acts from 1831 ensured that wages be paid in cash.

7 1 per cent plus 79 per cent copper and 20 per cent zinc.

8 It looks like a shark (Latin: *squalus* – a seafish).

9 Wrong. A slype is a covered passage, usually between the transepts and the chapter-house in a church, leading to the cloisters.

10 The *Great Britain*.

11 A Fifth Columnist. General Mola is reputed to have said that he had 'four columns encircling Madrid, and a fifth column working for him in the city'.

12 The Matterhorn.

Quiz Four

Answers

General Knowledge

1 Dogberry was a character in Shakespeare's *Much Ado About Nothing*, an ignorant, self-satisfied, overbearing, but good-natured night-constable.

2 Because Mendelssohn was not a Roman Catholic.

3 Lincoln.

4 The first florin, or 2/– coin, minted in 1849, without the words *Dei Gratia* – 'By the grace of God'.

5 The Fairey Swordfish, which, nevertheless, took its part in the sinking of the *Bismarck*.

6 Oak, bark, gall nuts and some other imported barks, as mimosa, acacia. It is used in the manufacture of leather, and writing-ink, and in medicine.

7 Queen Elizabeth I.

8 Castletown.

9 At Richmond, Yorkshire. It is a festival of drama and music held in September.

10 It is a Cistercian order which originated at the abbey of La Trappe in Normandy.

11 A Suffolk punch was (and still is) a beautiful short-legged thick-set cart-horse.

12 The rails on which a crane travels; also the area served by a crane.

Words

1 A fatal cattle disease (especially foot-and-mouth disease).

2 From the French, *crêpé*, meaning crinkly, which its surface is.

3 A legislature consisting of only one chamber of elected representatives.

4 To feel slighted, hence to take offence, to be overshadowed, to become insulted or angry. (From the Latin *umbra* – shadow.)

5 It is a collection of versions in different languages of the same work, especially the Bible. Also a person who speaks several languages.

6 Graphology.

7 It is an eyelet in a rope, sometimes lined with metal. Occasionally applied to a type of rowlock.

8 Place it upon a wound, boil, carbuncle, etc. It is a poultice.

9 Put it on your head. It is an early form of wig. 'Peruke' became 'periwig', periwig became 'wig'.

10 It is the right of fishing in another's waters, in common with the owner, and possibly others.

11 It would depend upon your taste. A sorosis is a compound fruit, consisting of many spores, e.g. the mulberry, blackberry, pineapple, etc. (Greek, *Soros* – a heap or cluster.)

12 To fade out of sight (vanish), to disappear.

Geography

1 John O'Groats (six main trunk routes – A1 to A6 – radiate from London, A7 – A9 radiate from Edinburgh).

2 Ripon.

3 Cavan, Donegal and Monaghan.

4 In Staffordshire about five miles north of Stoke-on-Trent.

5 The River Arun, on which Arundel stands.

6 It is a point near Meriden, Warwickshire, which is $72\frac{1}{2}$ miles equidistant from the Severn bridge, the Dee and Mersey estuaries and the Welland estuary on the Wash.

7 Two small rocky islands off Perranporth, Cornwall (also called the Bawon Rocks).

8 County Mayo, in Eire.

9 Inverness-shire.

10 Dun Laoghaire. (Dun Laoghaire actually means Leary's fort, which was built by a fifteenth-century king of that name.)

11 It isn't in Ireland. It is an island in the Inner Hebrides, 19 miles north-west of Iona.

12 County Dublin.

History

1 On the site of the modern Leadenhall market.

2 Only six.

3 Marylebone. Tyburn took the name of St Mary Le Bourne when a new church of St Mary was built there in the fifteenth century. It later became Maryborne and finally, due to popular etymology, Marylebone.

4 During the reign of the Roman Emperor, Hadrian (AD 117–138). (It did not reappear until the reign of Charles II, in 1665.)

5 The Whitefriars district, between Fleet Street, and the Thames. It afforded a sanctuary for debtors and law-breakers, a privilege derived from the Convent of Carmelites (Whitefriars) established there in 1241.

6 The London Stock Exchange met there for the first time as a separate body.

7 Norfolk (south side of the Wash) to Wiltshire (source of River Kennet, near Avebury).

8 Anglesey.

9 It is said to mark the burial place of Horsa, who, with Hengist, won a great victory over the Britons at Aylesford, on the Medway, five miles north-west of Maidstone, about AD 450. (Horsa was killed in the moment of victory and his grave was marked by a flint-heap, called horse-stead (Anglo-Saxon: *Horsa* – horse, *Stede* – place), around which the village arose.

10 Queen Anne, in 1711.

11 Skye.

12 The Macdonalds of Glencoe were killed by their hereditary enemies, the Campbells.

People

1 Sarah Bernhardt (1845–1923).

2 She was Norwegian.

3 Nijinsky (who was born seventy-seven years before his equine namesake).

4 Samuel Goldwyn, the famous US film producer (amongst other 'Goldwynisms' is: 'Anyone who visits a psychiatrist should have his head examined!').

5 Sherpa Tensing.

6 Master of the king's music(k).

7 She was the last Tzarina of Russia. She was murdered with the rest of the Russian Royal family at Ekaterinburg, in July 1918.

8 Peter (Ilich).

9 Spencer-Churchill.

10 He is his son. Duke of Rothesay is one of the subsidiary titles of the Prince of Wales.

11 He was Prime Minister of Canada from 1948–1957.

12 Stanley Baldwin, Conservative statesman and three times Prime Minister.

Literature

1 Giant Despair, according to John Bunyan in *Pilgrim's Progress*.

2 Joel Chandler Harris (1848–1908), the American author.

3 Angélique. Sergeanne Golon is the pseudonym of Serge Golon and Anne Golon.

4 Rabelais (1495–1553), in his great satire, *The History of Gargantua and Pantagruel*. Pantagruel, identified by some with Henry II of France, was son of Gargantua and the last of the giants.

5 Sir James Barrie in 1902.

6 'All for the sake of my little nut tree'.
I had a little nut tree, nothing would it bear,
But a silver nutmeg and a golden pear;
The King of Spain's daughter came to visit me,
And all for the sake of my little nut tree.

7 She answered: '*Then what about kilts?*'

8 George Bernard Shaw, in *Man and Superman.*

9 Cortez, the Spanish explorer.

10 *On first looking into Chapman's Homer.*

11 George Meredith (1828–1909).

12 Oliver Goldsmith, in Johnson's *Epitaph on Goldsmith.*

Sports and Pastimes

1 Berlin.

2 Joe Louis, the famous American heavyweight boxer.

3 Men compete at indoor tennis.

4 Four and a quarter inches.

5 Coursing. The Waterloo Cup, the 'Derby' of the coursing fraternity in which hares are coursed by greyhounds.

6 One – Billy Wright. William Ambrose Wright, CBE, has played in thirty-eight international championships, and sixty-seven foreign international and World Cup matches.

7 It is a run scored when the ball has glanced off any part of the batsman's person except his hand, provided he has made a stroke at the ball.

8 Baseball: he was the famous 'Babe Ruth'.

9 Dumfries.

10 Third Lanark.

11 Billiards. The balk line is a line drawn across the table twenty-nine inches from the bottom cushion. A ball is said to be in balk within this space.

12 Rugby Union has fifteen players in each team, Rugby League eleven.

Music

1 As a Coronation Ode for Edward VII.

2 Sibelius.

3 To a string player: with the mute. To a pianist: with the damper, or soft pedal. (Also used by brass players.)

4 It was one of the earliest of bowed instruments, and one of the ancestors of the violin family. The tenor rebec is still played in Greece and Crete to this day.

5 At Bayreuth in Bavaria.

6 *Mezzo* means half, e.g., *mezzo-soprano* is a voice half-way between soprano and contralto. *Mezzo forte* is half-loud.

7 A semibreve. (Our breve, rarely used now, is a double whole-note. A crotchet is a quarter-note.)

8 A quaver (not a crotchet!). The French names stand alone as being purely descriptive of the appearance of the notes, the quaver resembling a hook, the semi-quaver, a double hook (*croche, crochet*-hook), because of the tail or tails which hang down from quavers and notes of lesser value.

9 *Coppélia.*

10 Igor Stravinsky.

11 George Frederick Handel.

12 *Don Juan* or *Don Giovanni.* (The full title is *Il Dissoluto Punito, Ossia Don Giovanni.*)

General Knowledge

1 After pubs with the sign of Cupid.

2 Louisiana.

3 It is the coagulated, or thickened, part of milk (the watery part is whey).

4 St George slaying the dragon.

5 Macaroni are round and have holes in them (tubes). Fettucini are flat.

6 They are the green pickled flower buds of the caper bush, which grows in Sicily, North Africa, Majorca and other Mediterranean countries.

7 It is the candied root of the angelica plant, but can also be the stalk or stem.

8 Fruit and vegetables.

9 The eye.

10 Thirty years.

11 He would have lived there. It was a circular tower, a Scottish iron-age chieftain's stronghold, for farming, and the occasional highway robbery. (Also, in Scotland, a luminous ring round the moon popularly regarded as a sign of bad weather.)

12 The gauge is 4 ft. $8\frac{1}{2}$ ins., as it is also in most of Europe, Canada, and the USA.

Quiz Five   Answers

General Knowledge

1 The bittern. (The etymology is dubious, but may be from its booming note which is said to resemble the lowing of a bull.)

2 They govern the country. The Skutpshtina is the Jugoslav Parliament, or General Assembly.

3 It is the breast-bone, which runs down the front of the body from the neck to the stomach.

4 A small fresh-water fish. The word is a simple corruption of stickleback.

5 Chelsea, 1745.

6 Pimento.

7 An Ecclesiastical Court – the Court of Appeal for the Province of Canterbury and also, since 1874, of the Chancery Court of the Province of York.

8 A blow for a blow – tit for tat.

9 Roland and Oliver were two knights of Charlemagne, and their exploits were so similar that it was difficult to tell them apart. What Roland did, Oliver did, and the other way round. In the end, the two met in single combat, and fought for five consecutive days on an island in the Rhine. But so well-matched were the pair that the outcome was a draw.

10 The Northern diver, or loon. (Called the ember goose because it appeared on the coast about the time of the Ember Days in Advent.)

11 Tokyo – Osaka (the train covers the 320-mile distance at a speed of 130 mph).

12 It was a piece of strong tarred cloth strung across pit tunnels – or 'roads' – to minimise the effect of gas or blast from explosion.

Words

1 One who is not a gipsy to a gipsy. (Gorgio – corruption of gorgies meaning non-gipsy.)

2 In a carpenter's shop. Scobs are shavings or sawdust.

3 Eruption: bursting out (like a volcano, for instance); irruption: rushing in. Also used in the sense of invasion.

4 It is the nautical term for a spar set diagonally from the mast to extend a fore-and-aft sail.

5 A small and usually dry watercourse, except after the rains.

6 The first: early: primitive.

7 A scaly ant-eater of tropical Asia and Africa. It is a toothless mammal which uses its long slender tongue to capture insects.

8 A whole number, or undivided quantity as opposed to a fraction. (A whole or entire thing or entity.)

9 A dried sausage made of meat partly cooked. (The meat should be pork.)

10 Pleased. Eupepsia means having a good digestion – as opposed to dyspepsia.

11 It is a light Indian bedstead.

12 A candidate, especially for admission to a religious order.

Geography

1 On (the left bank of) the River Hooghly – the most westerly mouth of the Ganges – about eighty miles from the Bay of Bengal.

2 It is a twin-city community of Texas and Arkansas, with the state boundary line running through the middle of it.

3 In northern Spain. They provide the hinterland to the north coast of Spain, from the north of Portugal, almost to the western end of the Pyrenees.

4 Alaska: 586,400 square miles. (Texas: 267,339 square miles, California: 158,693 square miles.)

5 Turin (Torino).

6 Rhodesia and Zambia.

7 Omdurman.

8 Zomba.

9 In southern Turkey.

10 The Cyclades.

11 You'd hardly believe it, but it's Nord.

12 Cuba and Haiti.

History

1 *Speedwell.*

2 Philadelphia.

3 Newfoundland. It became the first English colony anywhere, when Sir Humphrey Gilbert formally took possession in 1583. The first colony in what is now the USA was Virginia, found by Raleigh in 1584, probably on Roanoke Island.

4 1 July 1867.

5 Delaware (because it was the first to ratify the Federal Constitution in 1787).

6 Franklin D. Roosevelt (1932, 1936, 1940, 1944). He died 12 April 1945.

7 Spencer Perceval. He was Prime Minister from 1809 until May 1812, when he was assassinated by a bankrupt madman.

8 Calais, in 1558.

9 Fiji.

10 King William IV's wife, Queen Adelaide.

11 Godwin, Earl of Kent and Wessex. He was Edward the Confessor's strongest pro-English Minister. In his time, the sands were a low-lying island called Lomea (the Roman *Infera Insula*), which was inundated about AD 1100.

12 James II when Duke of York. (He received the grant of what was then called New Netherland from his brother Charles II, in 1664.)

People

1 No. Because Giacomo Agostini is a world champion motor-cyclist.

2 The Duke of Gloucester.

3 Fifty-two (1564–1616).

4 The Duke of Norfolk, Earl Marshal of England.

5 Dame Lilian Baylis. She was made a CH in 1929.

6 Bing Crosby.

7 Cary Grant.

8 Clara Bow. She epitomised the 'flapper of the jazz age' of the 1920s and, significantly, her film career did not really survive that hectic decade.

9 Judy Garland.

10 The West German Chancellor, Herr Willy Brandt.

11 Joseph Conrad (1857–1924). His full name was Josef Feodor Konrad Nalecz Korzeniovsky.

12 Earl Kitchener of Khartoum.

Literature

1 *Rupert of Hentzau* (1898).

2 The imaginary country of 'Ruritania', which has since become a word in the English language.

3 *In the spring a livelier iris changes on the burnished dove.*

4 In Spenser's *Faerie Queene*. Sansfoy is the 'Faithless', Sansjoy, the 'Joyless' and Sansloy, the 'Lawless'. Some contend that they have a political connotation.

5 Thackeray's *Henry Esmond* (1852). She is the mother of Beatrix and the widow of the second Lord Castlewood, in this novel.

6 *At Flores in the Azores*
   Sir Richard Grenville lay.

7 He commanded the flagship the *Revenge* and was killed off Flores
   in 1591 when he attacked Spanish treasure ships.

8 *Le Morte d'Arthur*, dealing with the exploits of King Arthur's
   Knights of the Round Table.

9 Tennyson, who entitled it: *In Memoriam, A.H.H.*, but it is now
   better known simply as *In Memoriam*.

10 John Keats. (Keats died 1821 – *Adonais* written 1821).

11 He was a hardware merchant.

12 Henry James.

Sports and Pastimes

1 Norwich City (from their yellow shirts).

2 Clyde Walcott, Everton Weekes and Sir Frank Worrell.

3 Newmarket.

4 Both boats sank. (The race was re-rowed later, and Oxford won.)

5 He would be spearing salmon or other fish by torchlight, probably
   illegally.

6 The West Indies play cricket.

7 Australians play cricket. The Sheffield Shield is awarded annually
   to the winner of the inter-state cricket competition.

8 Mah-jong. They are the five suits in this Chinese game.

9 Lacrosse.

10 The contest for Doggetts Coat and Badge – a sculling contest for
   Thames watermen, dating from 1716.

11 The All-England Croquet Club, in 1875.

12 They are all well-known winter-sports centres – Arosa in
   Switzerland, Chamonix in France and Lillehammer in Norway.

Music

1 The biblical son of Cush was Nimrod, 'the Mighty Hunter before the Lord'. Elgar's Ninth Enigma variation is marked 'Nimrod' and was a tribute to A. J. Jaeger, of Novello and Co. 'Jaeger' or 'Jäger' is the German for hunter, hence the allusion to Nimrod.

2 The cello.

3 Benjamin Britten (first produced in Venice, 1954).

4 *La Tosca.*

5 A *nocturne.* (Literally, *Nachtstück* means a night piece, the German equivalent of *nocturne.*)

6 The Unfinished Symphony.

7 He never heard it performed. The Ninth Symphony was not completed until 1824 and Beethoven became totally deaf in 1819. (It was actually first performed in Vienna.)

8 Thirty-two.

9 One hundred and four.

10 Honegger, Milhaud, Poulenc, Durey, Auric, and Tailleferre.

11 The player of a wind instrument in an orchestra.

12 Lionel Bart.

General Knowledge

1 Leningrad. World renowned for its wide boulevards and beautiful buildings. The main thoroughfare of Leningrad is called the *Nevsky Prospekt.*

2 Originally called *Staaten Landt* by Tasman in 1642, it was later renamed *Nieuw Zeeland*, after the Dutch province of Zeeland.

3 He makes cutting and shaping dies.

4 None. The anna does not exist any more. The Indian units of currency are a hundred paisa to one rupee.

5 2 per cent.

6 20/–. Officially fixed at 21/– in 1717.

7 The edelweiss. The clue was 'alpinum', signifying a mountain flower.

8 Yellow.

9 The chrysanthemum. (It is the floral emblem of the Imperial family of Japan.)

10 The scarlet pimpernel, because it closes its petals on the approach of rain.

11 The rhododendron.

12 The Amazon river.

Quiz Six

General Knowledge

1 The fork.

2 It is a Parliamentary constituency of Liverpool.

3 Devonport.

4 The late Leslie Howard.

5 Aluminium.

6 In Plymouth.

7 The redundance or repetition. Avon is Welsh for 'river': Nyasa is Swahili for 'lake': so 'River Avon' means 'River River': and 'Lake Nyasa' means 'Lake Lake'.

8 Lake Malawi (since 1965).

9 In a ballet. An entrechat is a vertical jump into the air, during which the feet are repeatedly crossed and uncrossed. (Nijinsky – the ballet dancer, not the horse! – is said to have been able to cross and uncross his feet seven times whilst in the air.)

10 *Peahens* lay eggs; peacocks don't!

11 False. The oak-apple is an excrescence caused by the grubs of the minute gall-wasp, which lays its eggs in the oak tree. The true fruit is the acorn.

12 To convert a rotary motion into a to-and-fro one, e.g. in pumps and steam-engine valves.

Words

1 A crossbow-man would have sent an arrow through it. They were narrow apertures, or loopholes in the walls of a castle, sometimes in the form of a cross, through which crossbow-men discharged their arrows.

2 An arbalester was another name for a crossbow-man (Latin, *arcus* – bow, and *ballista* – an engine of war for throwing missiles).

3 It is an ecclesiastical council, or meeting, e.g., the synods of the provinces of Canterbury meet three times a year to form the convocation of the Church of England.

4 There isn't any difference. A paragon is a model or pattern, a type of excellence of perfection – and so is a paradigm.

5 You would not like it at all. A pseudologer is a calculating and systematic liar.

6 Business ('Pidgin English' is 'Business English').

7 A lych was a corpse.

8 Lawful. The opposite of illicit.

9 It is long-suffering, or forbearance or patience.

10 Yes, he was. An eponym is someone who gives his name to something; frequently something he invents or discovers, in this case the unit of electrical resistance. Ampère and Volta are similar examples.

11 A tinkling of bells (from the Latin *tintinnabulum* – a bell).

12 Originally, a left-handed baseball player, especially a pitcher.

Geography

1 It originates in the Gulf of Mexico, but it derives its impetus by being banked up by the easterly trade winds and forced to flow north-east up the American coast until it escapes their influence around the Grand Banks off Newfoundland, about latitude 45°–50°N, whence it flows across the Atlantic to north-east Europe.

2 They are two volcanoes on the island of Hawaii. Mauna Loa is active, Mauna Kea extinct. (Mauna Kea, from its base on the sea-bed to its summit, is 33,476 ft high – about 4,450 ft higher than Everest. From sea-level it is 13,796 ft.)

3 Albania.

4 In the south-west corner of France. (Roughly from the Pyrenees to the River Gironde, and as far east as the Central Massif.)

5 The Oder and the Neisse. The Neisse runs into the Oder about thirty miles south of Frankfurt-an-der-Oder, about eighty miles east-south-east of Berlin.

6 The Niagara. Between lakes Ontario and Erie and separating New York State from the province of Ontario.

7 The Main (Frankfurt-am-Main), which runs into the Rhine at Mainz, just south of Wiesbaden.

8 Curacao, Aruba, Bonaire, off the Venezuelan coast, and Saba, St Eustatius and part of St Martin, in the Leeward Islands.

9 On the Zambesi, near Livingstone (on the border between Zambia and Rhodesia).

10 It is an area of semi-desert plateau, in Cape Province, South Africa. In spite of its aridity, sheep are grazed on the low grey-green shrub, or Karroo bush, which grows there.

11 Lusaka.

12 The north and south islands of New Zealand.

History

1 No one. Priam was the last King of Troy.

2 There was no Colosseum in Nero's time. His successors, the Emperors Vespasian, Titus and Domitian, built the Colosseum on the site of Nero's lake in AD 72–80; Nero died in AD 68.

3 The Huns – and the man was Attila, their king. They were a savage race of Asian nomads, probably of Mongolian or Tartar stock, who overran the Middle East and Europe from Persia to the Rhine.

4 They were identical! In 27 BC Octavian was given the title Augustus (Venerable) and was known by that name thereafter.

5 The north of Scotland.

6 On the Island of Crete, and neighbouring islands.

7 Nineveh.

8 Dionysus I, Ruler of the Greek colony of Syracuse in the fifth century BC, because he got sick of being told that the life of the governing class was all beer and skittles.

9 Roxana, daughter of King Oxyartes of Bactria (Afghanistan), *c.* 329 BC. He later married Barsine, daughter of Darius, about 324 BC, the year before he died.

10 The Cynics.

11 After a disastrous naval defeat by Octavius, at Actium in 31 BC, both Antony and Cleopatra committed suicide.

12 Bath. *Aquae Sulis* means the Waters of Sul (a Roman deity). From the hot springs there, which the Romans made into baths.

People

1 The Carmelites, because of their white cloaks.

2 Dr Hewlett Johnson, from 1931 to 1963. He gained the dubious title because of his avowed communism – in the best sense of the word – and his support of Anglo-Soviet friendship.

3 Queen Elizabeth the Queen Mother. (Princess Margaret was also born there.)

4 A clergyman.

5 Joe Frazier, the heavy-weight boxing champion of the world.

6 Edgar Wallace (1875–1932).

7 Wystan Hugh.

8 A marital one. They were married in 1950.

9 They are all American astronauts.

10 The first Christmas card.

11 Champagne. (Although the Marquis de St Evremond, who was exiled to London in the seventeenth century, is said to have found the secret of making champagne some twenty years earlier.)

12 They were both great ballet dancers of their day: Marie Camargo, 1710–70, was one of the first great dancers (she shortened her skirts to mid-leg, then considered indelicate, so that her precise foot movements could be seen); Fanny Elssler, 1810–85, came from Vienna, and perfected point dancing.

Literature

1 Greece – in Athens and in a wood near it.

2 Miranda.

3 Autolycus. A character in *The Winter's Tale*.

4 He was a carpenter.

5 Caliban.

6 Daedalus, who tried to teach his son, Icarus, literally to fly from Crete, when banished by King Minos. As you know, Icarus finished up 'in the drink when his wings packed up' – as they say in the RAF.

7 Duke of Milan. His title was usurped by his brother, Antonia.

8 Because it was written to be performed on Twelfth Night. (The first record we have of the play being acted was on 6 January 1602 before the court at Whitehall by the Lord Chamberlain's company to which Shakespeare belonged.)

9 In *King Henry IV, Part II*. They are described by the author as 'country soldiers'.

10 Sir John Falstaff, Edward Poins, Bardolph, Pistol and Peto.

11 Britain.

12 *All's Well That Ends Well*.

Sports and Pastimes

1 In the cricket field. Victor Thomas Trumper was an Australian batsman who played forty-eight times for his country.

2 At Henley – they are events in the Henley Royal Regatta.

3 Basketball.

4 Playing baseball.

5 None. The American (and French) game of billiards is confined to cannons.

6 Judo.

7 Freddie Trueman. He took 307 wickets between June 1952 and June 1965.

8 Twenty-two yards.

9 Captain Matthew Webb. He swam from Dover to Calais in just under twenty-two hours in 1875.

10 He means a bogey – the accepted lowest score for a hole or course.

11 Knur and spell was a primitive form of cricket. It was played with a knur – a wooden ball, and a tripstick or bat, and the spell was a kind of trap roughly corresponding to the wicket.

12 On a fencing foil. The button is on the point – to prevent its causing injury, the foible is the lower half of the blade, the forte is the upper half of the blade, and the cushion is within the guard.

Music

1 Handel, born 1685. (Haydn, 1732; Mozart, 1756; Beethoven, 1770; Schubert, 1797; Mendelssohn, 1809.)

2 Paul Dukas, the French composer. (Original title: *L'Apprenti Sorcier*.)

3 It is the third note of any major or minor scale. So called as being midway between the tonic (key-note) and the dominant (fifth).

4 B natural. B flat is called B by the Germans.

5 *The Lass that Loved a Sailor*.

6 *Fidelio*, by Beethoven.

7 Mozart (Symphony No. 41, in C Major).

8 Ko-Ko.

9 *Peter Grimes*, by Benjamin Britten.

10 *Parsifal*, completed in 1882. Wagner died in Venice in 1883.

11 It is a realistic movement (some might say onomatopoeic) in his oratorio, *Israel in Egypt*.

12 Mendelssohn.

General Knowledge

1 In Rangoon.

2 A Chinese temple (or house for idol worship). A joss is a Chinese idol, or cult image.

3 St Crispin.

4 The goat.

5 Taurus, the bull.

6 The secretary bird, so called from the resemblance of the tuft of feathers at the side of its head to a quiver of pens behind a Victorian secretary's ear. It does catch and eat poisonous snakes.

7 Rocking stones. Stones so delicately poised by nature that they will rock to and fro at a touch. There are many in Yorkshire, Derbyshire, Wales and Cornwall, and are believed to have had some Druidical significance. (When the logan rock, about 70 tons, at Land's End was displaced by a naval lieutenant in 1824, he was ordered to replace it. His prank was a costly one, for the replacement cost £2,000 – say £20,000 today.)

8 False. Fernando Po is a Portuguese island off the south coast of Nigeria in the Gulf of Guinea. Selkirk was marooned on Juan Fernandez, about 400 miles west of Chile, in the South Pacific, whence Dampier did, in fact, rescue him five years later.

9 Battery Sergeant-Major.

10 The Artful Dodger (in *Oliver Twist*).

11 The national epic of the Finns.

12 Osaka, in Japan.

Quiz Seven

General Knowledge

1 It is the poison fang on a snake, so called because it is sickle-shaped. (The name is also applied to part of the brain.)

2 It is a spider-like insect but not a true spider. It feeds on other insects and dead animals.

3 Frog-hoppers are small brown insects which leap a considerable distance when touched. The larvae, known as froth-flies, surround and protect themselves with a mass of froth, called cuckoo-spit.

4 The May bug; or in some countries, the June bug or beetle.

5 It is a small bird, something like the hedge sparrow, about seven inches long, which frequents rocky mountain slopes in Spain, France, Italy, Greece and Yugoslavia.

6 Aardvark. The ant-bear of central and southern Africa.

7 The house martin is a bird like a swallow. The rest are mammals.

8 It is a beautiful, black and white, silky-haired West African monkey, with a long and pendulous tail, which almost literally flies between the top branches of forest trees.

9 A fine (twelve-pointed) stag, set in the Scottish Highlands.

10 They are all breeds of pig.

11 A pole or rudder.

12 A pea-chick.

Words

1 Funeral rites, or a funeral procession.

2 It is a shorthand sign representing a whole word.

3 Smallpox.

4 Your pronunciation. Orthoëpy is the correct pronunciation of words. (Greek, *Ortho* meaning right, *Epos* meaning word.)

5 It is a plant – a weed of the genus *fumaria*, but some varieties are cultivated.

6 Écru. It means 'unbleached' in French.

7 Willy-nilly. Willing or not willing.

8 It is from the Old English 'ceap-mann', a merchantman or tradesman. Cheapeman became chapman, which was abbreviated to chap. So a good, honest, travelling chapman became a good chap, or a good fellow.

9 You would be hopping mad! Nescient means ignorant.

10 One which cannot be mixed. Like oil with water.

11 Sorry. Pedicular means lousy. (Latin *pediculus* – louse).

12 He would be most annoyed. Oscitation means yawning.

Geography

1 The River Avon, which rises in the Cotswolds and flows through Bath and Bristol to the River Severn at Avonmouth.

2 The River Usk.

3 Elgin (the county was formerly called Elginshire).

4 Belfast.

5 Largely rest, quiet enjoyment and recreation. It is a 64-acre park in south-east London.

6 The Faroe Islands (between Iceland and the Shetlands), belonging to Denmark.

7 Fair Isle, which has given its name to knitted goods of a multi-coloured design.

8 In County Durham. It is a village about six miles south-west of Sunderland.

9 Lincolnshire.

10 The River Mersey.

11 Lancashire and Cheshire.

12 The Isle of Arran.

History

1 Ivan the Terrible. (He was crowned Czar or Emperor of Russia in 1547. Until then, the rulers of what was then Russia had been known as Grand Dukes.)

2 The Countess Markievicz (formerly Constance Gore-Booth, 1868–1927). She was a militant Irish Nationalist, sentenced to death for her part in the Easter Rebellion of 1916, reprieved, and elected to Parliament as a *Sinn Fein* member in 1918, but refused to take her seat. (The first woman MP to take her seat in the House of Commons was Lady Astor, representing Plymouth in 1919.)

3 Edward V; and his brother the Duke of York.

4 King Henry V in 1420.

5 Henry VI was the son of Henry V and Catherine of Valois. After the death of Henry V in 1422, Catherine secretly married Owen Glendower, by whom she had a son, Edmund Tudor, later first earl of Richmond, who became the father of Henry VII.

6 All Souls College, unique because it has no students. (It was founded by Archbishop Chichele as a chantry where masses should be said for the souls of those killed in the wars of Henry V and Henry VI.)

7 Nicholas Breakspear, or Pope Adrian IV, the only English Pope. He crowned Barbarossa in 1155 (he also had a row with England's Henry II about the sovereignty of Ireland).

8 William the Conqueror in 1078. He built what is known as the White Tower, on the site of a fort erected by Julius Caesar.

9 King James I, in 1611, who sold the title for £1,000 a time, for the maintenance of troops in Northern Ireland.

10 Earl of Leicester.

11 The Isle of Man (in Manx-Gaelic).

12 Vice-Admiral.

People

1 The late Kenneth Horne, Richard Murdoch and Sam Costa.

2 She was the favourite wife of Mahomet and lived *c*. 613–678.

3 Bathsheba. Formerly the wife of Uriah the Hittite: and after King David had engineered Uriah's death, the wife of David himself.

4 Herod Antipas.

5 Robert Louis Stevenson. So called by the Samoans, when he settled in that island in 1888.

6 On the new decimal coinage. Mr Machin designed the portrait of the Queen on the obverse of the coins, and Mr Ironside, the reverse designs.

7 They have all had their facsimile signatures on Bank of England notes, as chief cashiers of the Bank.

8 King Edwin of Northumbria, who built a fort there about AD 617, Edwin's Burg, hence Edinburgh.

9 'Publish and be dammed'.

10 For his founding of McGill University, in Montreal, in 1821 (chartered in 1821, opened in 1829).

11 HM The Queen.

12 The Duke of Edinburgh.

Literature

1 George Bernard Shaw. The first words of the *Aeneid* are: *Arma Virumque Cano*, meaning: 'Arms and the Man, I sing'. *Arms and the Man* was written by Shaw.

2 Sir Arthur Conan Doyle. *The Song of the Bow* appears in the novel, *The White Company*.

3 Johann Wyss (1781–1830), a Swiss professor at the University of Berne.

4 Fyodor Dostoevsky (1921–81).

5 Peter Cheyney (1896–1951).

6 Alexandre Dumas, the Elder (1802–70).

7 Sir Walter Scott (1771–1832). It is on the River Tweed, near Melrose.

8 *Gentlemen Prefer Blondes*.

9 Rudyard Kipling (1865–1936). It was awarded to him in 1907 and was England's first Nobel Prize in literature.

10 Robert Louis Stevenson (1850–94).

11 They were the owners of the house called 'The Franchise', in the best-selling novel and film, *The Franchise Affair* by Josephine Tey. In the book the empty house was eventually set on fire by arsonists.

12 'Dapple'.

Sports and Pastimes

1 The Royal Flush: ace, king, queen, knave, 10 of the same suit.

2 It is from the Persian, *shah-mat*, meaning 'the king is dead'. (The phrase in its present form is Arabic but the Arabic is derived from Persian.)

3 The sacrifice of a pawn or other minor piece, in order to build up a strong attacking position. (Also a remark or comment to launch a conversation – or make a telling point, a tactical move or manoeuvre.)

4 *Passe* is any number between nineteen and thirty-six. (*Manque* is one to eighteen.)

5 A wooden staff or sword. Kendo is a Japanese style of fighting with wooden swords – or staffs.

6 If you were attacked. Aikido is a form of Japanese unarmed combat, a technique midway between judo and karate.

7 Malls were the mallets used in the game of 'Pall-Mall' popular in Charles II's reign, when the walk, now called 'The Mall', was appropriated to it for the use of the King and his court. (Presumably the import of Monk's order was to ensure that the malls were not used for more belligerent purposes.)

8 It is a colloquialism for the shuttlecock.

9 From Badminton House, in Gloucestershire, the seat of the Dukes of Beaufort, where it was first played in the late 1860s.

10 Lacrosse.

11 144 pieces or tiles.

12 A circle was traced around a mark in the centre. All playing knelt round the circumference and each pitched a coin as near as he could to the centre mark, the one getting his coin nearest having the right of tossing all the coins in the air together, keeping those which came down head uppermost.

Music

1 *No, No, Nanette* by Vincent Youmans.

2 Sir Edward Elgar, in 1900.

3 *Here's to the Next Time.*

4 The cello.

5 The cornet. As solo cornettist with various American jazz bands in the 1920s, eventually with Paul Whiteman, he became a legend in the jazz world of his day. He died tragically at the age of 28.

6 Henry Purcell (*c.* 1658–95).

7 The piano. Cristofori called it a *Gravecembalo Col Piano E Forte* (a harpsichord with loudness and softness).

8 It is a passage in a concerto where the whole orchestra takes part (after a passage by the soloist). 'Tutti' (masculine plural of 'tutto') in Italian, means 'all', in the sense of 'all performers now take part'. In fact, it means 'all but one', for the soloist frequently takes a breather at this time.

9 Rossini, in his little-known opera *Othello*, now overshadowed by Verdi's *Otello*, written some sixty years later in 1877. Rossini's librettist, Berio, gave it Shakespeare's tragic ending, but when the opera reached Rome, in 1819, Rossini was asked to substitute a happy ending, which he did by inserting an aria from his earlier opera *Armida* sung by Othello and Desdemona after she has convinced him of her innocence.

10 Kurt Weill, with libretto by Berthold Brecht, in 1928. He called it *Die Dreigroschenoper* (it was a German version of Gay's *Beggars' Opera* with altered plot and new music).

11 A high-pitched oboe.

12 The 'G' string.

General Knowledge

1 It is another name for the song-thrush.

2 It is another name for the sea-eagle or white-tailed eagle, found largely in Iceland, parts of Scandinavia and Eastern Europe.

3 Three. A goosander is a fish-eating duck, similar to a merganser, about the size of a mallard (the smew is much smaller).

4 The stormy petrel (also called Mother Carey's chicken).

5 The peewit.

6 A turkey-cock (probably onomatopaeic).

7 It is a species of Indian stork, so called from its stately bearing.

8 In burrows (or rock cavities on northern islands) on cliffs and islets.

9 It is a type of finch, or species of linnet, found mostly in Ireland, Northern England, Scotland and the Eastern and Northern coasts of Scandinavia.

10 The corncrake. Like the other crakes and rails, very difficult to observe, as it differs from the perfect Victorian child by being more frequently heard than seen. Unlike the others of its species it frequents meadows, lush vegetation and crops rather than swamps and fens.

11 It is a large family of Australian birds, about the size of a thrush, with a slender pointed beak and divided tongue for sucking nectar and small insects from flowers.

12 The gannet. (*Solan* from old Norse, *Sula* – Iceland, where there are many of them.)

Quiz Eight

General Knowledge

1 Northumbria.

2 The River Tees.

3 Crimson.

4 The ribbon is white, with a broad violet central stripe.

5 St Luke's summer – it is the latter end of autumn.

6 A primitive bridge consisting of stone slabs laid across simple piers.

7 It is a white mark on the forehead of a horse.

8 No. You would chip off a piece of bark from trees bordering the trail, the white wood left showing being called a blaze; similar to the white mark on a horse.

9 The Cathedral Church of St John Lateran. (The basilica of St Peter's, Rome, is not classed as a cathedral.)

10 It is the device, composed of thin metal plates, by which the aperture of the lens can be varied.

11 Swiss francs.

12 It is a particularly venomous yellow viper of South America, with a head shaped like the metal head of a lance.

Words

1 Ferns.

2 It is Malayan for 'forest man'.

3 From *nap*hthalene and *palm* oil, of which it is a mixture.

4 A young animal, especially a young kangaroo, or a young child.

5 He would be interested in dogs (from the Latin *canis* – a dog, and the Greek *philein* – to love).

6 In a garden. It is a walk or terrace, sometimes covered, formerly of marble.

7 Cheiromancy is another name for palmistry, or telling fortunes from the lines of the hand.

8 It means to scale a wall with ladders. (From the Spanish: *escalada*, *escala* – ladder. Latin: *scala* – ladder.)

9 Yes. Scissile means capable of being cut.

10 One of the curved pieces in the circumference of a wheel, or the circular metal rim which surrounds it.

11 A cathode is a negative electrode (negative pole) and an anode is a positive electrode in an electrolytic cell or valve.

12 Palaeontology (or Fossilogy).

Geography

1 St Paul (it is the capital city of Minnesota).

2 Chicago. Because of the strong winds which blow off Lake Michigan.

3 The city of Dallas – Texas.

4 Philadelphia, Pennsylvania. Founded by a group of Quakers led by William Penn.

5 On the borders of Burma, South China, Thailand and Laos. Inhabited by the Shans, a Mongolian mainly Buddhist people, closely allied in language and custom with the Thais.

6 North Borneo.

7 The Tigris and the Euphrates.

8 Queensland (Australia) and New Guinea.

9 Finland.

10 Lesotho.

11 The Canary Islands.

12 Tierra del Fuego – the southernmost part of South America. It is an archipelago off the southern extremity of South America, partly Chilean and partly Argentine.

History

1 In 1912, on 13 May. (It became the RAF in 1918.)

2 An ensign (because he carried the ensign).

3 1914 (December).

4 The musket.

5 Oates, Wilson, Bowers and Evans.

6 1961 (April).

7 Georgi Maksimilianovich Malenkov.

8 Brother-in-law. Malenkov's second wife is Khrushchev's sister.

9 King Leopold I, favourite uncle of Queen Victoria.

10 General Batista.

11 Lord Halifax.

12 Warwick and Leamington.

People

1 Christopher Marlowe in a tavern in Deptford, apparently in a brawl over the bill, but probably owing to political intrigue.

2 The Archbishop of Canterbury.

3 A £1 treasury note. £1 and 10/– notes were issued by the Treasury from 1914–28, bearing the signature of J. S. Bradbury, Permanent Secretary to the Treasury, at the time. Subsequently all notes were issued by the Bank of England.

4 Aaron.

5 Esau.

6 Elizabeth, cousin of the Virgin Mary, wife of Zacharias.

7 It was initiated by Friedrich Wilhelm Froebel (1782–1852).

8 Formerly the Master of Revels, as at Christmas.

9 The same as the Lord of Misrule – in Scotland.

10 The Russian MiG fighters which they constructed.

11 The reflecting studs, encased in rubber, to show the middle and sometimes the sides of the road, in darkness.

12 Christian Dior.

Literature

1 Eugene O'Neill. He won the Nobel Prize for literature in 1936.

2 Tennessee Williams.

3 George Bernard Shaw.

4 Aristophanes.

5 *Adamant*.

6 Lewis Carroll.

7 It was the seat at the round table kept vacant for him who should find the holy grail.

8 Yes. Sir Galahad eventually did, after his successful quest for the grail.

9 He was a king of Cornwall, in the Arthurian legend, and husband of Isolde the Fair, who was 'passionately enamoured of' his nephew, Tristram.

10 They are both commonly called the Lady of the Lake.

11 Aeschylus (*c.* 525–456 BC).

12 W. S. Gilbert, between 1866 and 1871.

Sports and Pastimes

1 They were all one-time holders of the World one-mile running record in the 1930s.

2 Sir Henry Segrave, at Daytona Beach in 1926. In 1929, in his *Golden Arrow*, he raised it again to 231 mph.

3 The late Sidney Barnes, who took 49 wickets (in four matches) against South Africa in 1913–14.

4 Douglas Jardine. Formerly Captain of Surrey.

5 A Scottish football team of the Scottish Football Association. Its players are members of the Civil Service.

6 To score a 'duck' (nought) in each innings of a match.

7 (i) Preston North End, 1888–9; (ii) Aston Villa, 1896–7; (iii) Tottenham Hotspur, 1960–61.

8 Twenty-seven to twenty-eight inches.

9 Leeds United.

10 Twelve yards.

11 Pelota.

12 Twenty-two.

Music

1 Vaughan Williams (in 1910).

2 The Swiss composer, Arthur Honegger (1892–1955).

3 *The Merry Widow* by Franz Lehar.

4 Gaetano Donizetti (1797–1848).

5 They are the three Rhinemaidens in Wagner's opera *Das Rheingold*.

6 Serge Prokofiev (1891–1953).

7 Instrumental music descriptive of non-musical ideas. An example is Beethoven's *Pastoral Symphony*.

8 Rigoletto.

9 The polka or two-step.

10 Benjamin Britten.

11 George Frederick Handel (1685–1759).

12 The Marimba.

General Knowledge

1 Graf.

2 It is one of the best of the Sauternes.

3 One who obtains his booty free – hence a pirate, etc.

4 1981 – every ten years.

5 Sandhurst (St Cyr is a famous military Academy).

6 *Deo optimo maximo* (To God the best and greatest).

7 The Wednesday before Easter. (So called in an allusion to the betrayal of Christ.)

8 Mocha is a port of the Yemen from which the coffee was originally shipped.

9 In Arabia or north-east Africa. It is a hot, dry, dust-laden wind which passes in a few minutes.

10 46,000 tons.

11 Because the smoke passes through water, making a bubbling sound.

12 A natterjack is a species of toad with a yellow stripe running down its back. The stripe is a sort of camouflage as the toad inhabits sandy territory.

Quiz Nine

General Knowledge

1 The flat-topped, squat, circular defence towers which were erected along the coast of England during the threat of Napoleon's invasion, early in the nineteenth century. They were called 'Martello' towers, a corruption of 'Mortella' – where one such had proved, in 1794, very difficult to capture.

2 Lincoln Cathedral. (St Hugh, originally a Carthusian monk, later became Bishop of Lincoln. He lived from about 1140–1200.)

3 They are all British breeds of sheep.

4 They are all edible mushrooms.

5 He had committed Hara-Kiri, according to the time-honoured Japanese method of suicide. (Also suicide by disembowelment, as formerly practised by the higher classes in Japan.)

6 The principal work of the philosopher and mathematician René Descartes (1596–1650) which was published in 1637.

7 He is a hawker, especially of religious tracts and magazines.

8 During the American War of Independence, one of a body of militiamen ready to turn out at a minute's notice for service.

9 Off the Old Head of Kinsale, County Cork, Southern Ireland. About 20 miles south-west of Cork harbour.

10 No. Helsinki, the capital of Finland, was called Helsingfors in this country, and is still called so by the Swedes. Helsingör is a port on the north-east coast of Denmark, which Shakespeare called Elsinore, when he made it the setting for *Hamlet*.

11 The rowan tree, or mountain ash.

12 On an HMV or RCA Victor gramophone record. About 1900, Barraud first painted the picture of the dog listening to an Edison phonograph which was supposed to be reproducing the voice of its owner, and offered it to Edison. When he refused it, Barraud painted out the cylinder instrument and substituted a disc and horn one, and this was bought by its present proprietors, the Gramophone Co. Ltd.

Words

1 Possibly your gardening jacket. *Frazzle* is of American origin. It is an American expression for a frayed edge of, say, a sleeve.

2 It was another word for 'ifs'. Shakespeare used it frequently: e.g. 'An I were there', for 'If I were there', the verbal subjunctive mood indicating doubt.

3 As a noun, it meant the freight or cargo (of a ship). As a past participle of the verb, fraught, it meant filled or laden with cargo. (From old Dutch, *vracht*, or *vrecht* meaning freight.)

4 Adulterated (not in natural or original state).

5 It is a substance which, when introduced into other bodies, accelerates (or sometimes retards) a chemical reaction without undergoing change itself.

6 An eye for an eye; a tooth for a tooth. *Lex talionis* is Latin for the law of retaliation.

7 Quiet.

8 Jeopardy originally meant an even chance (from the French *jeu* meaning game; *parti* meaning divided). Later it came to mean an uncertain chance, something hazardous or even dangerous.

9 Sorry. A cacographer is a bad writer or speller. (From the Greek *kakos* meaning bad; *graphia* meaning writing.)

10 A dryad is a wood nymph. A naiad is a water or river nymph.

11 Books produced in the infancy of the art of printing, especially before the year 1500. (Also the earliest stages in the development of anything ornithological: the breeding-places of a species of bird.)

12 It is an incomplete document, e.g. an unsigned will or a signed cheque with the amount omitted.

Geography

1 Nebraska.

2 Nevada.

3 Boise.

4 The Paraguay river.

5 Rye. One of the additional Cinque ports.

6 Chile.

7 Only one – West Germany.

8 The Ivory Coast.

9 They are four provinces of communist China.

10 Somalia.

11 Sicily: 9,923 square miles, followed by Piedmont (9,817 square miles) and Sardinia (9,302 square miles).

12 The River Neva.

History

1 Oudenarde. Blenheim (1704), Ramillies (1706), Oudenarde (1708) and Malplaquet (1709) were the Duke of Marlborough's four famous victories in the War of the Spanish Succession.

2 King Charles II, from the name of his favourite racehorse. 'The Rowley Mile' at Newmarket is named after the same horse.

3 King Henry VIII. Although it was not until the Stuarts that this form of address became stereotyped.

4 King Charles I. Beheaded 30 January 1649. William III fractured his right collar-bone after being thrown from his horse in 1702, but when he died, a fortnight later, the cause was given as pleuro-pneumonia.

5 One granddaughter was Queen Mary, the wife of William III, and the other was Queen Anne. (They were daughters of Anne Hyde who was secretly married to James II when Duke of York.)

6 There isn't any connection! Hyde Park belonged originally to the Manor of Hyde which was attached to Westminster Abbey but which was taken by Henry VIII on the Dissolution of the Monasteries. It was opened to the public by James I in 1606 before Edward Hyde was born.

7 Franklin Delano Roosevelt in Hyde Park, New York, in 1882.

8 It is now generally accepted as between 1830 and 1832, during the struggle to pass the Reform Bill, although the cognomen had been used on occasions by speakers earlier than this.

9 At the same time as the Whigs became Liberals.

10 Henry 1. Because he was a good scholar (*Beau Clerc*), and could write more than his own name, a rare accomplishment for an aristocrat of his time.

11 Edward, the Black Prince, eldest son of King Edward III, created in 1337.

12 Tintagel. (According to Geoffrey of Monmouth in *Historia Britonium*.) The ruins of Tintagel castle, on the north coast of Cornwall, are mid-twelfth-century in origin.

People

1 Aneurin Bevan (1897–1960).

2 The international language called Esperanto.

3 The Rotary Club movement. Paul Harris was a Chicago lawyer who wished to promote the spirit of 'service to others' amongst American business and professional men. The first British Rotary Club was founded in 1911.

4 Detective Chief Superintendent Barlow and Detective Superintendent Watt. First in *Z Cars*, then *Softly, Softly*, and later in *Softly, Softly: Task Force*.

5 Sir Edwin Landseer (1802–73).

6 The Archbishop of York.

7 Also the Archbishop of York. The Archbishop of Canterbury is the Primate of All-England.

8 Glenda Jackson, for her performance in the film *Women in Love*.

9 Croesus, who lived in the fifth century BC.

10 Pandora.

11 Eurydice, whom he almost charmed back to life by his music.

12 A malevolent goblin who haunts forests, and lures people, especially children, to their death.

Literature

1 Charles Dickens wrote *Nicholas Nickleby* in one of the inns there.

2 *Rural Rides*.

3 Nancy. Murdered by Bill Sikes when it became known that she had tried to befriend Oliver.

4 George du Maurier, in 1894.

5 John Masefield (1878–1967).

6 T. S. Elliot (Nobel Prize 1948).

7 John Dryden (from 1670–1688). (Ben Johnson was granted a pension by James I, but he was never officially appointed.)

8 In the preface to *Pickwick Papers*, Dickens himself explains: 'It was the nickname of a pet child, a younger brother, whom I had dubbed Moses, in honour of the Vicar of Wakefield, which, being pronounced "Boses", got shortened into Boz.'

9 Laces or letters.
Laces for a lady,
Letters for a spy,
Watch the wall, my darling,
While the gentlemen go by.

10 Thoughtless open-handedness. She was typical of the enthusiastic, unthinking philanthropist who forgets that charity should begin at home.

11 Daphne du Maurier.

12 The tragic heroine of George Eliot's *The Mill on the Floss*.

Sports and Pastimes

1 1954 (on 6 May. Exact time was 3 mins 59·4 secs).

2 Christchurch, New Zealand, in 1974.

3 For the 400-metre race.

4 He was the heavyweight champion of the World from 1915–1919, when he was beaten by Jack Dempsey.

5 Twelve.

6 One point for every two wickets taken in the first thirty-five overs.

7 Lancashire.

8 The St Leger. 'The Classics', or the Classic Races, are the 2,000 guineas, 1,000 guineas, The Derby, The Oaks and The St Leger. The race is run at Doncaster in September.

9 Four and a half miles. (4 miles 856 yds, 24 yds short of $4\frac{1}{2}$ miles.)

10 He won the racing 'Triple Crown' – the three 'Classic' horseraces: Nijinsky was the first horse to achieve this great feat for thirty-five years.

11 They are all past Derby winners. Psidium: 1961; Larkspur: 1962; and Relko: 1963.

12 Because an archaic meaning of 'let' was to hinder or obstruct.

Music

1 'Satch-Mo' was a reference to Armstrong's mouth. 'Satch' means 'sack' or 'satchel', 'Mo' is short for 'mouth'.

2 *Madame Butterfly*, by Puccini. The reference is to Lieutenant Pinkerton of the US navy.

3 Sterbini wrote the libretto for Rossini's *Barber of Seville*.

4 Both are known as *The London Symphony*.

5 Sparafucile is a character in Verdi's Rigoletto. He is a hired assassin.

6 *The Witch's Curse – Ruddigore; The Peer and the Peri – Iolanthe; The Merryman and his Maid – The Yeoman of the Guard.*

7 Nine. It was published as No. 5 but is actually 9, Opus 95, *From the New World*, Symphony in E minor.

8 Michael Tippett.

9 Hawaii.

10 The *Appassionata*.

11 Sir Thomas Beecham (1879–1961).

12 The hornpipe.

General Knowledge

1 The 'V' stood for *Vergeltungswaffe* – Retaliatory (or vengeance) weapon.

2 They are both named after supposed Roman amphitheatres. The Colosseum in Rome was indeed the scene of gladiatorial contests and possibly chariot races. The Palladium, on the other hand, was a colossal wooden statue of Pallas, in the citadel of Troy, and upon which the safety of the city depended. It was carried away by the Greeks and later said to have been taken to Rome.

3 About nine hundred million people – a quarter of the world's population.

4 Prince Andrew.

5 The dukes of Devonshire.

6 In ancient Greece, a sacrifice of one hundred oxen.

7 Mississippi.

8 You probably would have run away. A morning star was a rather vicious weapon – a spiked iron ball on a stick which could crack any skull.

9 Stilton cheese (probably first developed at Kirby Bellars on the Melton Mowbray–Leicester Road).

10 The Paladins.

11 Bristol.

12 International Air Transport Association.

Two other popular quiz books based on BBC programmes

Ask the Family

Hundreds of questions to test your general knowledge. The book is divided into subject quizzes and covers a wide range of difficulty. Only a handful of people can appear on the BBC TV programme each season– but the book will provide hours of enjoyment for every family.

25p

Quiz Ball

Since 1966 when BBC TV's first *Quiz Ball* programme was shown, the majority of Britain's top soccer players have had the opportunity of showing their skill off the field by answering sporting and general knowledge questions. The book contains hundreds of questions (and answers) arranged so that Quiz Ball can be played at home.

30p